Routledge Revivals

The Substance of Faith Allied with Science

Originally published in 1907, this book provides information to parents and teachers wishing to teach their children about Christianity as well as science. Lodge details his fear of mandatory secularism in schools and advises how to instruct children in science without allowing any doubt of Christian doctrine and stresses the importance of reconciliation between religion and science for future generations. This title will be of interest to students of Education and Religion.

The Substance of Faith Allied with Science

A Catechism for Parents and Teachers

Oliver Lodge

Routledge
Taylor & Francis Group

First published in 1907
By Methuen & Co

This edition first published in 2016 by Routledge
2 Park Square, Milton Park, Abingdon, Oxon, OX14 4RN
and by Routledge
711 Third Avenue, New York, NY 10017

Routledge is an imprint of the Taylor & Francis Group, an informa business

Publisher's Note
The publisher has gone to great lengths to ensure the quality of this reprint but points out that some imperfections in the original copies may be apparent.

Disclaimer
The publisher has made every effort to trace copyright holders and welcomes correspondence from those they have been unable to contact.

A Library of Congress record exists under LC control number: 07009613

ISBN 13: 978-1-138-63911-9 (hbk)
ISBN 13: 978-1-315-63675-7 (ebk)
ISBN 13: 978-1-138-64026-9 (pbk)

THE SUBSTANCE OF FAITH

ALLIED WITH SCIENCE

A CATECHISM FOR PARENTS AND TEACHERS

BY

SIR OLIVER LODGE, F.R.S.

PRINCIPAL OF THE UNIVERSITY OF BIRMINGHAM

FIFTH EDITION

METHUEN & CO.
36 ESSEX STREET W.C.
LONDON

First Published	*February 1907*
Second Edition	*February 1907*
Third, Fourth, and Fifth Editions	*March 1907*

Gloriam quæsivit scientiarum, invenit Dei.

PREFACE

EVERYONE who has to do with children at the present day, directly or indirectly, must in some form or another have felt the difficulty of instructing them in the details of religious faith, without leaving them open to the assaults of doubt hereafter, when they encounter the results of scientific inquiry.

Sometimes the old truths and the new truths seem to conflict; and though everyone must be aware that such internecine warfare between truths can be an appearance only, the reconciliation is not easily perceived: nor is the task simplified by the hostile attitude adopted towards each other by some of the upholders of orthodox Christianity.

It is sometimes said to be impossible for a teacher to educate a class subject to compulsory attendance, in a spirit of weal-th, peace, and godliness, without infringing the legitimate demands of somebody; but the difficulty is caused chiefly by sectarian animosity, which may take a variety of forms.

These religious and educational disputes would be of small consequence, and might even be stimulating to thought and fervour, were it not that one danger is imminent:—a danger lest the nation, in despair of a happier settlement, should consent to a system of *compulsory* secularism; and forbid, in the public part of the curriculum of elementary schools, not only any form of worship, but any mention of a Supreme Being, and any quotation from the literature left us by the Saints, Apostles, Prophets, of all ages.

If so excentric a negation is brought about by the warfare of denominations, they will surely all regard it as a lamentable result.

Meanwhile, in the hope and belief that the great bulk of the teachers of this country are eager and anxious to do their duty, and lead the children committed to their care along the ways of righteousness,—being deterred therefrom in some cases only by the difficulty of following out their ideals amid the turmoil of voices, and in other cases by their uncertainty of how far the "old paths" can still be pursued in the light of modern knowledge,—I have attempted the task of formulating the fundamentals, or substance,[1] of religious faith in terms of Divine Immanence,[2] in such a way as to assimilate sufficiently all the results of existing knowledge, and still to be in harmony with the teachings of the poets and inspired writers of all ages. The state-

[1] "By Substance I understand that which exists in and by itself." (Spinoza.)

[2] "We may say much, yet not attain; and the sum of our words is, He is all." (Ecclesiasticus xliii. 27.)

ment is intended to deny nothing which can reasonably be held by any specific Denomination, and it seeks to affirm nothing but what is consistent with universal Christian experience.

Our knowledge of the Christian religion is admittedly derived from information verbally communicated, and from documents; and, in the interpretation of these sources, mistakes have been made. At one time, not long ago, it was the duty of serious students of all kinds to point out some of these mistakes, wherever they ran counter to sense and knowledge. That cleaning and sweetening work has been done vigorously, and done well: at the present time comparatively little sweeping remains to be done, save in holes and corners: most of the lost simplicity has now been found. A positive or constructive statement of religious doctrine, not indeed deduced from present knowledge, but in harmony with all that bears upon the subject, is now more useful. Such a statement might be called New Light on Old Paths; for the "old paths" remain, and are more brightly illuminated than ever: even the old Genesis story of man's early experience shines out as a brilliant inspiration. Truth always grows in light and beauty the more it is uncovered.

There are still people who endeavour to deny or disbelieve the discoveries of science. They are setting themselves athwart the stream, and trying to stop its advance;—they only succeed in stopping their own. They are good people, but unwise, and, moreover, untrustful. If they will let go their anchorage, and sail on in a spirit of fearless faith, they will find an abundant reward, by attaining a deeper insight into the Divine Nature, and a wider and brighter outlook over the destiny of man.

TABLE OF CONTENTS

REFERENCES TO QUOTATIONS

PAGE		
ix	"Old paths"	Jer. vi. 16.
13	"Hear no yelp"	Tennyson, "By an Evolutionist.
22	"Then welcome"	Browning, "Rabbi Ben Ezra."
22	"We fall to rise"	Browning, "Asolando."
23	"Nor shall I deem"	Browning, "Paracelsus."
30	"If my body"	Tennyson, "By an Evolutionist."
33	"Our wills"	Tennyson, "In Memoriam."
37	"The old order"	Tennyson, "Morte d'Arthur."
39	"Lilies that fester"	Shakespeare, Sonnet 94.
43	"All tended"	Browning, "Paracelsus."
44	"He hath shewed thee"	Micah vi. 8.
48	"The best is yet to be"	Browning, "Rabbi Ben Ezra."
49	"My son, the world"	Tennyson, "Ancient Sage."
50	"There shall never be"	Browning, "Abt Vogler."
51	"No ill no good"	Tennyson, "Ancient Sage."
55	"All we have willed"	Browning, "Abt Vogler."
59	"Where dwells enjoyment"	Browning, "Paracelsus."
59	"God tastes an infinite"	Browning, "Paracelsus."
65	"πάντα ῥεῖ καὶ οὐδὲν μένει"	Heraclitus.
	(Everything flows and nothing is stagnant.)	
65	"The hills are shadows"	Tennyson, "In Memoriam."
73	"πάντα πλήρη θεῶν"	Thales, quoted by Aristotle.
	(All things are full of gods.)	
73	"Earth's crammed"	E. B. Browning, "Aurora Leigh."
78	"Our birth"	Wordsworth, "Immortality."
81	"We are such stuff"	Shakespeare, "Tempest."
83	"Climb the mount"	Tennyson, "Ancient Sage."
86	"That none but Gods'	Tennyson, "By an Evolutionist."
87	"Flash of the will"	Browning, "Abt Vogler."
87	"All through my keys"	Browning, "Abt Vogler."
89	"'Tis the sublime"	Coleridge, "Religious Musings."
90	"Enough that he heard it"	Browning, "Abt Vogler."
101	"A sun but dimly seen"	Tennyson, "Akbar's Dream."
106	"But that one ripple"	Tennyson, "Ancient Sage."
110	"Signs of his coming"	Morris, "Love is Enough."
115	"Then stirs the feeling"	Byron, "Childe Harold."
115	"ἡ ψυχὴ τῷ ὅλῳ μέμικται"	Aristotle, "De Animâ."
	(Spirit permeates the whole.)	
115	"Whose dwelling"	Wordsworth, "Tintern Abbey."
124	"Their prejudice"	Browning, "Paracelsus."
126	"And we the poor earth's"	Tennyson, "Ancient Sage.

INTRODUCTION

THERE is a growing conception of religion which regards it not as a thing for special hours or special days, but as a reality permeating the whole of life. The old attempt to partition off a region where Divine action is appropriate, from another region in which such action would be out of place—the old superstition that God does one thing and not another, that He speaks more directly through the thunder of catastrophe or the mystery of miracle than through the quiet voice of ordinary existence—all this is beginning to show signs of expiring in the light of a coming day.

Those to whom such a change is welcome regard it as of the utmost importance that this incipient recognition of a Deity immanent in History and in all the processes of Nature shall be guided and elevated and made secure. Ancient formularies must be reconsidered and remodelled if they are to continue to express eternal verities in language corresponding to the enlarged acquaintance with natural knowledge now possessed by humanity.

Nevertheless the attempt to draw up anything of

the nature of a creed or catechism, unhallowed by centuries of emotion and aspiration, is singularly difficult; and to obtain general acceptance for such a production may be impossible.

Every Denomination is likely to prefer its own creed or formula, especially if it has the aroma of antiquity upon it—an aroma of high value for religious purposes and more easily destroyed than replaced. No carefully drawn statement can be expected to go far enough to satisfy religious enthusiasts: it is not possible to satisfy both scientific and distinctively denominational requirements. All this might be admitted, and yet it may be possible to lay a sound foundation such as can stand scientific scrutiny and reasonable rationalistic attack—a foundation which may serve as a basis for more specific edification among those who are capable of sustaining a loftier structure.

Even though not yet fully attainable, it is permissible to hope for more union than exists at present among professing Christians, and among the branches of the Christian Church. With some excellent people the differences and distinguishing marks loom out as of special importance; but from these I can hardly claim attention. I must speak to those who try to seize points of agreement, and who long for the time when all Christian workers may be united in effort and friendliness and co-operation, though not in all details of doctrine. On the practical side, a concurrence of effort for the amelioration and spiritualisation of human life, in the light of a common gospel and a common hope, is not impossible; and on the theoretical side, in spite of legitimate differences of belief on difficult and infinite problems, there must be a mass of fundamental material on which a great majority are really agreed.

But a foundation is not to be mistaken for superstructure: a full-fledged and developed religion needs a great deal more than foundation—there must be a building too. The warmth and vitality imparted by strong religious conviction is a matter of common observation, and is a force of great magnitude; but it is a personal and living thing, it cannot be embodied in a formula or taught in a class. Here lies the proper field of work of the Churches. What can be taught in a school is the fundamental substratum underlying all such developments and personal aspirations; and it can be dealt with on a basis of historical and scientific fact, interpreted and enlarged by the perceptions and experiences of mankind.

A creed or catechism should not be regarded as something superhuman, infallible, and immutable; it should be considered to be what it really is—a careful statement of what, in the best light of the time, can be regarded as true and important about matters partially beyond the range of scientific knowledge: it must always reach farther into the unknown than science has yet explored.

An element of mystery and difficulty is not inappropriate in a creed, although it may be primarily intended for comprehension by children. Bare bald simplicity of statement, concerning things keenly felt but imperfectly known, cannot be perfectly accurate; and yet every effort should be made to combine accuracy and simplicity to the utmost. Every word should be carefully weighed and accurately used: mere conventional terminology should be eschewed. A sentence stored in the memory may evolve different significations at different periods of life, and at no one period need it be completely intelligible or commonplace. The ideal creed should be profound rather than explicit, and yet should convey some sort of meaning even to the simplest and most ignorant. Its terms, therefore, should not be technical, though for full comprehension they would have to be understood in a technical or even a recondite sense.

To make a statement of this kind useful, it is necessary to accompany each clause with some indication of the supplementary teaching necessary to make it assimilable: and such hints should be adapted not only to professed teachers, but to parents and all who have to do directly or indirectly with the education of children. It is my hope that the following clauses and explanations may be of some use also to the many who experience some difficulty in recognising the old landmarks amid the rising flood of criticism, and who at one time or another have felt shaken in their religious faith. Some of them are sure to have attained emancipation and conviction for themselves, but in so far as their own insight has led them in the general direction indicated by what follows, these will not be the last to welcome an explicit statement, even though in several places they may wish to modify and amend it. They will recognise that there is an advantage, for some purposes, in throwing old and over-familiar formulæ into new modes of expression; and that a variety in mode of formulation does not necessarily indicate a lack of appreciation of the loftiest truths yet vouchsafed to humanity.

With these preliminary remarks I now submit a catechism, whereof the clauses are intended to be consistent with the teachings of Science in its widest sense, as well as with those of Literature and Philosophy, and to lead up to the substance or substratum of a religious creed.

I

THE ASCENT OF MAN

Q. What are you?

A. I am a being alive and conscious upon this earth; a descendant of ancestors who rose by gradual processes from lower forms of animal life, and with struggle and suffering became man.

CLAUSE I

This answer does not pretend to exhaust the nature of man; another aspect is dealt with in Clause XII. It is usual to impart the latter mode of statement first; but premature dwelling on the more mystical aspect of human nature, with ignorance or neglect of the biological facts actually ascertained concerning it, only gives rise to troubled thought in the future when the material facts become known —often in crude or garbled form — and leads to scepticism.

The clause as it stands is a large and comprehensive statement, that will need much time for its elucidation and adequate comprehension. Its separate terms may be considered thus:—

EARTH.—Children can gradually be assisted to realise the earth as an enormous globe of matter, with vast continents and oceans on its surface and with a clinging atmosphere, the whole moving very rapidly (nineteen miles each second) through space, and constituting one of a number of other planets all revolving round the sun. They may also be led to realise that from the distance of a million miles it would appear as an object in the sky rather like the moon; that from a greater distance it would look like any of the other planets; while from a vastly greater distance neither it nor any other planet is large or luminous enough to be visible—nothing but the sun would then be seen, looking like a star. It is occasionally helpful to realise that the earth, with all its imperfections, is one of the heavenly bodies.

BEING.—The mystery of existence may be lightly touched upon. The fact that anything whatever—even a stone—exists, raises unanswerable questions of whence and why. It is instructive to think of some rocks as agglomerations of sand, and of sand as water-worn fragments of previous rock; so that, even here, there arises a sense of infinitude.

ALIVE.—The nature of life and, consequently, of death is unknown, but life is associated with rapid chemical changes in complex molecules, and is characterised by the powers or faculties of assimilation, growth, and reproduction. It is a property we share with all animals and also with plants. Children should not be told this in bald fashion, but by judicious questioning should be led to perceive the essence of it for themselves. Soon after they realise what is meant by life, some of them will perceive that it has an enormous range of application, and will think of flowers as possessing it also: being subject like all living things to disease and death.

What plants do not possess is the specifically animal power of purposed locomotion, of hunting for food and comfort, with its associated protective penalty of pain.

CONSCIOUS.—Here we come to something specially distinctive of higher animal life. Probably it makes its incipient appearance low down in the scale, in vague feelings of pain or discomfort, and of pleasure; though it is not likely that worms are as conscious as they appear to us to be. In its higher grades consciousness means awareness of the world and of ourselves, a discrimination between the self and the external world—"self-consciousness" in its proper signification: an immense subject that can only be hinted at to children. They can, however, be taught to have some appreciation of the senses, or channels, whereby our experience of external nature is gained; and to perceive that the way in which we apprehend the universe is closely conditioned by the particular sense-organs which in the struggle for existence have been evolved by all the higher kinds of animal life,—organs which we men are now beginning to put to the unfamiliar and novel use of scientific investigation and cosmic interpretation. What wonder if we make mistakes, and are narrow and limited in our outlook!

Digression on the Senses

Our fundamental interpretative sense is that of touch—the muscular sense generally. Through it we become aware of space, of time, and of matter. The experience of *space* arises from free motion, especially locomotion; *speed* is a direct sensation; and *time* is the other factor of speed. Time is measured by any uniformly moving body—that is by space and speed together. Muscular action impeded, the sense of *force* or resistance, is another primary sensation; and by inference from this arises our notion of "matter," which is sometimes spoken of as a permanent possibility of sensation. Hardness and softness, roughness and smoothness, are all inferences from varieties of touch. Another sense allied to touch is that of *temperature*, whereby we obtain primitive ideas concerning heat. Then there are the chemical senses of taste and smell; and lastly, the two senses which enable us to draw inferences respecting things at a distance. These two attract special attention; for the information which they convey, though less fundamental than that given by the muscular sense, is of the highest interest and enjoyment.

The ear is an instrument for the appreciation of aerial vibrations, or ripples in the air. They may give us a sense of harmony; and in any case they enable us to infer something concerning the vibrating source which generated them, so that we can utilise them, by a prearranged code, for purposes of intelligent communication with each other—a process of the utmost importance, to which we have grown so accustomed that its wonder is masked.

The eye is an instrument for appreciating ripples in the ether. These are generated by violently revolving electric charges associated with each atom of matter, and are delayed, stopped, and reflected in various ways, by other matter which they encounter in their swift passage through the ethereal medium.

From long practice and inherited instinct we are able, from the small fraction of these ripples which enter our eyes, to make inferences regarding the obstructive objects from which they have been shimmered and scattered. It is like inferring the ships and boats and obstacles in a harbour from the pattern of the reflected ripples which cross each other on the surface of the water.

The precision and clearness with which we can thus gain knowledge concerning things beyond our reach, and the extraordinary amount of information that can be thus conveyed, are nothing short of miraculous: though, again, we are liable to treat sight as an everyday and commonplace faculty. We are not, however, directly conscious of the ripples, though they are the whole exciting cause of the sensation; our real consciousness and perception are of the objects which have invested the ripples with their peculiarities, have imprinted upon them certain characteristics, and made them what they are. The eye is able to analyse all this, as the ear analyses the tones of an orchestra.

ANCESTORS.—In the first instance *human* ancestors may be considered, and a family tree drawn for any one child; from which he will learn how large a number of persons combine to form his ancestry. The tree can also represent the converging effect of inter-marriages, so that ultimate descent from a common ancestor is not an impossibility, if the facts of biology and ethnology point in that direction—as it appears they do. The probable though remote relationship existing between all the branches of the human family may be suggested by an inverted tree descending from some remotest ancestor: for whom Noah is as good a name as any other.

ROSE.—The doctrine of the ascent of man may be found in some cases to conflict with early religious teaching. If so, offence and iconoclasm should be carefully avoided; and if the teacher feels that he can conscientiously draw a distinction, between the persistent vital or spiritual essence of man, and the temporary material vehicle which displays his individual existence amid terrestrial surroundings, he may with advantage do so. The second or higher aspect of the origin of man is dealt with in Clause XII. The history and origin of the spiritual part of man is unknown, and can only be rightly spoken of in terms of mysticism and poetry: the history of the bodily and much of the mental part is studied in the biological facts of evolution.

The doctrine of the ascent of man, properly regarded, is a doctrine of much hope and comfort. Truly it is an unusual item in a child's creed; but it is, I think, a helpful item: it explains much that would otherwise be dark, and it instils hope for the future. For in the light of an evolution doctrine we can readily admit—(1) that low and savage tendencies are naturally to be expected at certain stages, for an evanescent moment; and (2) that having progressed thus far, we may anticipate further —perhaps unlimited—advance for mankind.

The fact that each individual organism hastily runs through, or reduplicates, a main part of the series of stages in the life-history of its race, is a fact of special interest and significance; notably in connection with the trials and temptations of human beings during their effort to cleanse away the traces of animal nature. The severity of the contest is already lessening, and both the individual and the race may look forward to a time when the struggles and failures are nearly over, when the unruliness of passion is curbed, when at length we

> ". . . hear no yelp of the beast, and the man is quiet at last
> As he stands on the heights of his life with a glimpse of a
> height that is higher."

GRADUAL PROCESSES.—The slowness and precariousness of evolution may be indicated; and the possibility of descent or degeneration, as well as of ascent and development, must be insisted on. A genealogical tree can be drawn laterally, to illustrate the origin of any set of animals—both those risen and those fallen in the scale—from some, possibly hypothetical, common ancestor. The dog on the one hand, and the wolf or jackal on the other, may serve as easy examples of ascent and descent respectively, and of relationship between higher and lower species, or even genera, without direct or obvious connection. The horse and the bear may serve as examples of distant relationship; birds and reptiles as another; and we may point out that at each stage of inheritance some of the progeny may ascend a little in the scale, and some descend a little.

Presently the sponge of time may wipe out the common ancestry at the root of the lateral tree, and nothing be left but some of its ascending and some of its descending branches,—all suited to their environment and so continuing to live and flourish, each in its own way; but so apparently different, that relationship between them is a matter of inference, and is sometimes difficult to believe in. The example of the caterpillar and butterfly, however, of the tadpole and the frog, etc., can be used to remove incredulity at extraordinary and instructive transmutations—transmutations which in the individual represent rapidly some analogous movements of racial development in the history of the distant past. The degradation of certain free-swimming animals, such as ascidians, which in old age become rooted or sessile like plants, can be pointed to as typical, and, indeed, a true representation of what has gone on in a race also, during long periods of time The rapid passage of the embryo through its ancestral chain of development should be known, at any rate to the teacher; and in general the greater the teacher's acquaintance with natural history, the more living and interesting will be the series of lessons that can occasionally be given on this part of the clause.

The popular misconception concerning the biological origin of man, that he is descended from monkeys like those of the present day, is a trivial garbling of the truth. The elevated and the degraded branches of a family can both trace their descent from a parent stock; and though the distant common ancestor may now be lost in obscurity, there is certainly in this sense a blood relationship between the quadrumana and the bimana: a relationship which is recognised and is practically useful in the investigations of experimental pathology.

LOWER FORMS OF ANIMAL LIFE.—The existence of single cells and other low microscopic forms (like amœbæ), and the analysis or dissection of a more complex structure (say rhubarb) into the cells of which it is in a sense composed, together with some indication of the vital processes occurring in similar but isolated cells (such as yeast or protococcus) which lead us to consider them as possessing life—of a form so fundamental that there is in some cases no clear discrimination between animal and vegetable—may be spoken of and exhibited in the microscope.

From a not very different-looking minute germinal vesicle, or nucleus of a cell, the chick is developed.

The lower forms of animal life, spoken of in the clause as ancestral, may be understood to go back to forms even as low as these,—indeed, to the lowest and minutest forms which in dim and distant ages can have possessed any of the incipient characteristics of life at all: down, perhaps, to some unknown process whereby the earthy particles began to coalesce under a vivifying influence. And as the race springs from lowly forms of cell life, so does the individual,—the body of each individual was once no more than a microscopic cell-nucleus or germinal vesicle. Therein was the germ of life: and the complex aggregate of cells we now possess has all been put together by the directive power latent in, or initially manifested by, that germ. So it is also with a seed—an apple pip, an acorn, or a grain of mustard seed.

But there are many forms of animal life not in the direct line of our ancestry—side branches, as it were, of the great terrestrial family. At present the earth is dominated by man, but at one time it was mastered by gigantic reptiles, larger than any land creature of to-day, the remains of which are occasionally found fossilised into stone and embedded in the rocks; fit to be collected and preserved in museums.

For millions of years the earth was inhabited by creatures no higher than these; the progress upwards has been slow and patient: time is infinitely long, and the great history of the world is still working itself out.

Still do lower forms exist side by side with higher; and many of them are suited to their surroundings, and in their place are beautiful and sane and perfect of their kind. But a few of the lower forms are lower because they have failed to reach the standard of their race, they are very far from any kind of perfection, they are at war with their environment; and for these, the only alternatives are extinction or improvement. In such a species as man the variety or range of achievement and of elevation is enormous. Among men and their works we find, on the one hand, cathedrals and oratorios and poems, and faith and charity and hope; on the other, slums and ugliness and prisons, and spite and cruelty and greed. And we must not forget that want of harmony with environment may in some cases be the fault, not of the individual, but of the environment: a fault which it is specially likely to possess when man-made. For every now and then is born an individual far above the average of the race, amid surroundings which he finds deadly and depressing. He may be despised and rejected by his fellows, and nevertheless may be the precursor or herald of a nobler future.

The problem, the main human problem, is how to deal with the earth now—now that we have at length attained to conscious control—so as to cease perpetuating the lower forms, and to encourage the production of the higher; by giving to all children born on the planet a fair chance of becoming, each in its own way, a noble specimen of developed humanity.

STRUGGLE AND SUFFERING.—Children should realise the bleak and unprotected state through which their remote ancestors must have begun a human existence, the great dangers which they had to overcome, the contests with beasts and with the severities of climate, the hardships and perils and straits through which they passed; and should be grateful to those unknown pioneers of the human race, to whose struggles and suffering and discoveries and energies our present favoured mode of existence on the planet is due.

The more people realise the effort that has preceded them and made them possible, the more are they likely to endeavour to be worthy of it: the more pitiful also will they feel when they see individuals failing in the struggle upward and falling back towards a brute condition; and the more hopeful they will ultimately become for the brilliant future of a race which from such lowly and unpromising beginnings has produced the material vehicle necessary for those great men who flourished in the recent epoch which we speak of as antiquity; and has been so guided, since then, as to develop the magnificence of a Newton and a Shakespeare even on this island in the northern seas.

II

THE DEVELOPMENT OF CONSCIENCE

Q. 2. *What, then, may be meant by the Fall of man?*

A. At a certain stage of development man became conscious of a difference between right and wrong, so that thereafter, when his actions fell below a normal standard of conduct, he felt ashamed and sinful. He thus lost his animal innocency, and entered on a long period of human effort and failure; nevertheless, the consciousness of degradation marked a rise in the scale of existence.

CLAUSE II

This clause has been inserted because of the historic, though often mistaken, notions accreted round a legend of Fall and of a Paradise lost; and it is of interest to detect the germ of truth which these ancient ideas contain. It may be regarded as really an appendage of, or introductory to, the next clause.

The sense of guilt and shame is to some extent displayed by a dog; but it appears to be due to domestication, and to be a secondary result of human influence. In any case, it is certainly only the higher animals that thus exhibit the germ of conscience, and the sense of shame and remorse: a sense which is most real and genuine when it is independent of externally inflicted and of expected punishment. Wild animals appear to have no such feeling, they glory in what we may picturesquely speak of as their "misdeeds," and in running the gauntlet of danger to achieve them; and though often cruel, they are free from sin. Some savages—our own Norse forefathers among others—must on their freebooting expeditions have been in similar case. So were some of the Homeric heroes. It would be only the highest and most thoughtful among them that could rise to the sense of guilt and degradation. Only those who have risen are liable to fall. The summit of manhood is attained when evil is consciously overcome. The period before it was recognised as such has been called the golden age; but the condition of unconsciousness of evil, though joyous, is manifestly inferior to the state ultimately attainable, when paradise is regained through struggle and victory.

Mere innocency, the freedom from sin by reason only of lack of perception, is not the highest state; it has been thought ideal from the point of view of inspiration and poetry, but it is a condition in which advance is necessarily limited. Sooner or later fuller knowledge and consciousness must arrive; and then ensues a long period of discipline and distress, until first a Leader and ultimately the race find their way out, through temptation and difficulty, once more to freedom and joy.

A perception that the possibility of backsliding is a necessary ingredient in the making of man, and the consequent discernment of a soul of goodness in things evil, constitute a large part of the teaching of Browning:

> "Then welcome each rebuff
> That turns earth's smoothness rough,
> Each sting that bids nor sit nor stand, but go!
> Be our joys three parts pain!
> Strive to hold cheap the strain;
> Learn, nor account the pang: dare, never grudge the throe."

And again—

> "We fall to rise, are baffled to fight better,
> Sleep to wake——"

The intervening period between fall and victory, between loss of innocency and gain of righteousness, is the period with which all human history is concerned : and there is often a corresponding period in the life-history of every fully developed individual, during which he gropes his way through darkness and longs for light.

Immense is the area still to be traversed and illumined: only faint gleams penetrate the dusk. A Light has indeed shone through the darkness, but the darkness comprehended it not. The race itself is still enveloped in mist, and only here and there a glint of reflexion heralds the brightness of a coming dawn. Yet a time will come when we shall cast away the works of darkness and put upon us the armour of light, and stand forth in the glory of completed manhood:

> "Nor shall I deem his object served, his end
> Attained, his genuine strength put fairly forth,
> While only here and there a star dispels
> The darkness, here and there a towering mind
> O'erlooks its prostrate fellows. When the host
> Is out at once, to the despair of night,
> When all mankind alike is perfected,
> Equal in full-blown powers—then, not till then,
> I say, begins man's general infancy."

III

CHARACTER AND WILL

Q. 3. *What is the distinctive characteristic of man?*

A. The distinctive character of man is that he has a sense of responsibility for his acts, having acquired the power of choosing between good and evil, with freedom to obey one motive rather than another.

Creatures far below the human level are irresponsible; they feel no shame and suffer no remorse; they are said to have no conscience.

CLAUSE III

In putting this question, children may be asked to suggest characteristics which distinguish man from animals. If gradually they hit upon clothes and fire and speech they will do well.

Clothes may be defined as artificial covering removable at will; "artificial" meaning made by an artificer, or manufactured, as opposed to natural growth, like fur. But the changes of covering among animals should not be overlooked: moulting for instance, renewal of skin necessitated by growth, protective change of colour at summer and winter, and so on.

The discovery of *Fire* is a thing to be emphasised, because familiarity with lucifer matches is liable to engender contempt for this great pre-historic discovery. People should realise that at one time the production of flame *de novo* was extremely difficult: the ordinary method of lighting fires being to keep some one fire always alight, so that brands could be ignited at it and thus it could be spread. The fact that lighting other fires does not diminish or weaken the original stock, is noteworthy, and is an analogy with life which may be typified by oaks and acorns—any number of trees arising from a parent stock, and spreading for innumerable generations. The ancient ceremony of keeping flames alight on sacred altars was doubtless due to the difficulty of re-ignition when every fire in a village had accidentally become extinguished. That the ancients valued fire highly, and felt strongly the difficulty of generating it, is shown by the legend that the first fire must have been stolen from heaven; and the priests taught, as usual in barbarous times, that the gods were jealous and angry at man's discoveries and the progress of science.

Speech and *language* is a most vital characteristic of manhood, and is largely responsible for the chasm between him and other animals. The gestures and noises of animals must not be overlooked, however, and they often seem to have mysterious modes of communication of some kind. But they have nothing akin to *writing*, and this portentous discovery enables not merely communication between contemporary living men, but an accumulation of information and experience throughout the centuries; so that a man is no longer dependent solely on his own individual experience, but is able to draw upon the records and wisdom of the past. Owing to this power of recording and handing on information, a discovery once made becomes the possession of the human race henceforth for ever—unless it relapses into barbarism.

WILL

None of these characteristics, however, is emphasised in the clause, because they lead too far afield if pursued. For our present purpose we regard the sense of "conscience," suggested by the previous answer, as the most important and highest characteristic of all,—the sense of responsibility, the power of self-determination, the building up of character, so that ultimately it becomes impossible to be actuated by unworthy motives. Our actions are now controlled not by external impulses only, but largely by our own characters and wills. The man who is the creature of impulse, or the slave of his passions, cannot be said to be his own master, or to be really free; he drifts hither and thither according to the caprice or the temptation of the moment, he is untrustworthy and without solidity or dignity of character. The free man is he who can control himself, who does not obey every idea as it occurs to him, but weighs and determines for himself, and is not at the mercy of external influences. This is the real meaning of choice and free will. It does not mean that actions are capricious and undetermined; but that they are determined by nothing less than the totality of things. They are not determined by the external world alone, so that they can be calculated and predicted from outside: they are determined by self and external world together. A free man is the master of his motives, and selects that motive which he wills to obey.

If he chooses wrongly, he suffers; he is liable also to make others suffer, and he feels remorse. In a high grade of existence no other punishment is necessary. Artificial punishment has for its object the production of artificial remorse, in creatures too low as yet for the genuine feeling. Artificial punishment can be easily exaggerated and misapplied, and should be employed with extreme caution. It is always ambitious and often dangerous, though sometimes justifiable and necessary, to attempt to take the place of Providence. Even between parents and children, enforcement of another's will may be overdone, till the power of self-control and the instinct of duty are impaired.

The sense of responsibility inevitably grows with power and knowledge, and is proportional thereto. By means of drugs a grown man may enfeeble his will till he becomes in some sense irresponsible for his actions; but he is not irresponsible for his wilful destruction of a human faculty; and in so far as he is dangerous to others he must be treated accordingly.

The struggle in man's nature between the better and the worse elements,—sometimes spoken of as a struggle between dual personalities, and otherwise depicted as a conflict between the flesh and the spirit,—is a natural consequence of our double ancestry (spoken of in Clause XII.), our ascent from animal fellow-creatures, and our relationship with a higher order of being. No man in his sober senses really wills to do evil: he does it with some motive which he tries to think justifies it; or else he does it against his real will because mastered by something lower. So Plato teaches in the *Gorgias.* And St. Paul says the same thing:

"The good which I would, I do not; but the evil which I would not, that I do."

The conflict is often a period of torment and misery. "O, wretched man that I am! who shall deliver me from the body of this death?"

Whenever the better nature prevails in the struggle, there is a mystic sense of strength and comfort universally testified to by humanity, even though the victory results in temporal loss or persecution; "in all these things we are more than conquerors." And this fact corresponds with part of the answer to Question 6 below.

We can recognise that our evil impulses are the natural remnant of bestial ancestry, and need not be due to diabolical promptings. An animal, though perhaps innocent from lack of knowledge, is bound and enslaved by its instincts; for instance, the apparently intelligent and social bee is driven by racial instincts into a prescribed course of action; a cat can no more refrain from trying to catch a bird than a man of high nature can allow himself to commit a crime.

The weak man often allows his brute nature to get the upper hand and enslave his higher self, and he hates himself afterwards for the degradation so caused; but the strong and free man takes control, and dominates his animal nature.

"If my body come from brutes, tho' somewhat finer than their own,
I am heir, and this my kingdom. Shall the royal voice be mute?
No, but if the rebel subject seek to drag me from the throne,
Hold the Sceptre, Human Soul, and rule thy Province of the brute."

IV

DUTY AND SERVICE

Q. 4. *What is the duty of man?*

A. To assist his fellows, to develop his own higher self, to strive towards good in every way open to his powers, and generally to seek to know the laws of Nature and to obey the will of God; in whose service alone can be found that harmonious exercise of the faculties which is identical with perfect freedom.

CLAUSE IV

The laws of nature signify the ascertained processes and consistencies observable in all surrounding things; they are a special and partial, but accurately ascertainable, aspect of what is called the will of God. They cannot be broken or really disobeyed; but we may set ourselves in fruitless antagonism to them,—as by building a bridge too weak to stand, by various kinds of wrong conduct, eating unduly or wrong kind of food, by careless sanitation and neglect of health. But all such ignorance or neglect of the laws of nature involves disaster. By knowing them, and acting with them, we show wisdom; and by steady persistence in right action we attain the highest development possible to us at present; we also escape that dreary sense of disloyal hopeless struggle against circumstances which is inconsistent with harmony or freedom. So long as the will of any creature is antagonistic to the rest of the universe, it is not fully developed. There must be a harmony among all the parts of a whole; but in the case of free beings it is not a forced but a willing harmony that is aimed at; and all experience takes time

> "Our wills are ours, we know not how,
> Our wills are ours to make them Thine."

The higher a man can raise himself in the scale of existence—by education, right conduct, and persistent effort—the more he may be able to help his fellows. To some are given ten talents, to some five, and to another one; but it is the duty of all to use their talents to the uttermost, so that they may fulfil the intention of the higher Power which brought us into existence and intrusted us with responsible control. Events do not happen without adequate cause, and in so far as agents, stewards, or trustees rest on their oars or misuse their opportunities, improvements now possible will not be accomplished. We must regard ourselves as instruments and channels of the Divine action; even in a few things we must be good and faithful servants, and it is our privilege to help now in the conscious evolution and development of a higher life on this planet.

The race of man has far to travel before it can be regarded as an efficient organ of the Divine Purpose. The extremes of ability and character and virtue are widely separated; and the occasional elevation of a leader, here and there, serves but to display the darkness in which the majority of a race so newly evolved are still imprisoned; crawling feebly toward the light, in a state of only rudimentary consciousness; anxious about trivialities, opposing and hindering instead of helping each other, competing rather than co-operating, fighting and struggling and killing in the throes of racial birth. It is often difficult to realise the possible perfectness of human life, in the midst of so much difficulty and discouragement.

And much of the difficulty is unnecessary and artificial. Deficiency in the means of subsistence, or in modest comfort, is not a reasonable condition of human life. The earth is ready to yield plenty for all, and will when properly treated and understood; but never will it spoil its children with bounties from a neglected breast. It must be coaxed and coerced, and then it will respond lavishly. We expend plenty of energy already, only we misapply it. If only our aim could be changed, and our energy be concentrated on clear and conscious pressing forward, with a definite mark in view — towards which all could work together and all together could attain, instead of one at the expense of others—" then would the earth put forth her increase, and God, even our own God, would give us His blessing."

(The "duty" clauses in the Church Catechism are well worth learning.)

V

GOODNESS AND BEAUTY AND GOD

Q. 5. *What is meant by good and evil?*

A. Good is that which promotes development, and is in harmony with the will of God. It is akin to health and beauty and happiness.

Evil is that which retards or frustrates development, and injures some part of the universe. It is akin to disease and ugliness and misery.

CLAUSE V

"Development" means unfolding of latent possibilities; as a bud unfolds into a flower, or as a chicken develops from an egg.

The idea controlling this answer is that growth and development are in accordance with the law of the universe, and that destruction and decay are features which are only good in so far as they may be on the way to something better; as leaf-mould assists the growth of flowers, or as discords in their proper place conduce to, or prepare for, harmony. In the same way conditions and practices which once were good become in process of time corrupt; yet out of them must grow the better future.

> "The old order changeth, yielding place to new,
> And God fulfils Himself in many ways,
> Lest one good custom should corrupt the world."

The law of the Universe, and the will of God, are here regarded as in some sort synonymous terms. It is impossible properly to define such a term as "God," but it is permissible reverently to use the term for a mode of regarding the Universe as invested with what in human beings we call personality, consciousness, and other forms of intelligence, emotion, and will. These attributes, undoubtedly possessed by a part, are not to be denied to the whole; however little we may be able as yet to form a clear conception of their larger meaning.

It is quite clear that the Universe was not made by man; it must owe its existence to some higher Power of which man has but an infinitesimal knowledge. Some primary conception of such a Power has been independently formed by every fraction of the human race, and is what under various symbols has been called God.

It is sometimes asserted that God does not possess powers and faculties and attributes which we ourselves possess. But that is preposterous: for though we may be able to form no conception as to the particular form our powers would take, when possessed by a being even moderately higher in the scale of existence than ourselves; and although vastly more must be attributed to the Reality denoted by the term "God" than we can even begin to conceive of; yet such a term, if it is to have any meaning at all, must at least include everything we have so far been able to discover as existent in the Universe. It must, in fact, be the most comprehensive term that can be employed; though for practical purposes it may be permissible to discriminate, and exclude from its connotation, portions such as "self," and "the world," and sometimes, though with less excuse, even an abstraction like "nature"; considering these separately from the more purely personal aspect to which attention is directed by our ordinary use of the term God. It is convenient to differentiate the principle of evil also, and to reserve it for separate study.

Sometimes the totality of existence is spoken of as the "Absolute," and the term God is limited to the conception of a Being of infinite Goodness and Mercy, the ultimate Impersonation of Truth and Love and Beauty; a Being of whose attributes the highest faculties and perceptions of man are but a dim shadow or reflexion.

In man, goodness is the path toward higher development, and a radiant beauty is the crown and perfection of life; so the trinity of Truth, Goodness, and Beauty, often referred to in literature, may, without undue stretching, be considered as also equivalent to what is represented by the words, the Way, the Truth, and the Life; they are three aspects of what after all is one essential unity. That which is good, in the highest sense, cannot help being both true and beautiful. Nevertheless, for many practical purposes, these ideas must be discriminated; and the question is occasionally forced upon our attention whether vitality or beauty can possibly be enlisted in the service of evil; and if so, whether it is still in itself good.

We have to learn that most good things can be misapplied, and that though they do not in themselves cease to be good, their desecration is especially deadly. That the corruption of the best abets the cause of the worst, is proverbial; the prostitution of high gifts to base ends is the saddest of spectacles.

"Lilies that fester smell far worse than weeds."

Oratory, the power of persuasion, can thus be debased, and the passions of the multitude may be incited by the Divine fire of eloquence. Rhetoric and sophistry have been on this ground condemned when they were misused for the cultivation of the art of persuasion apart from knowledge and virtue; but almost every good gift—personal affection, medical science, artistic genius—has every now and then been abused; and the higher and nobler the faculty, the more sorrowful and diabolical must be its prostitution.

It has been an ancient puzzle to consider whether the principle of goodness is the supreme entity in the universe—a principle to which God as well as man is subject—or whether it represents only the arbitrary will of the Creator. Many answers have been given, but the answer from the side of science is clear:—

No existing universe can tend on the whole towards contraction and decay; because that would foster annihilation, and so any incipient attempt would not have survived; consequently an actually existing and flowing universe must on the whole cherish development, expansion, growth: and so tend towards infinity rather than towards zero. The problem is therefore only a variant of the general problem of existence. Given existence, of a non-stagnant kind, and ultimate development must be its law. Good and evil can be defined in terms of development and decay respectively. This may be regarded as part of a revelation of the nature of God.

VI

MAN PART OF THE UNIVERSE

Q. 6. *How does man know good from evil?*

A. His own nature, when uncorrupted by greed, is sufficiently in harmony with the rest of the universe to enable him to be well aware in general of what is a help or hindrance to the guiding Spirit, of which he himself is a real and effective portion.

CLAUSE VI

We are not something separate from the Universe, but a part of it: a part of it endowed with some power of control—power to guide ourselves and others and assist in the scheme of development—power also to go wrong, to set ourselves contrary to the tendency of things, to delay progress, and break ourselves in conflict with overpowering forces.

When not thus warped or misled, we fit into the general scheme, and, like all other portions of existence, can fulfil our function and take our due share in the general progress. We are a part of the Universe, and the Universe is a part of God. Even we also, therefore, have a Divine Nature and may truly be called sons and co-workers with God. The consciousness of this constitutes our highest privilege, and likewise our gravest responsibility. Perception of this is dawning with increasing brightness on the human race in the light of the doctrine of evolution. The process of evolution has no end: progress is toward an advancing goal. At one time

> "... all tended to mankind,
> And, man produced, all has its end thus far:
> But in completed man begins anew
> A tendency to God."

We are essential and active agents in the terrestrial order of things, analogous to the white corpuscles in the human body. The body may be regarded as a colony of cells, some of which are living and moving on their own account; in complete ignorance of the feelings and perceptions of the larger whole of which they are microscopic units, towards whose health and comfort nevertheless they unconsciously but very really contribute; it is in fact by their activity that the health of the body is maintained against adverse influences. So it is with the health of the body politic, to which our wise activity is necessary and essential; we are to be a corporate portion of the whole, effective servants of the guiding and controlling Spirit. But in our case it is not merely unconscious service that is called for: we are privileged not only to be servants, but friends; not only to work, but to sympathise; to give not only dutiful but affectionate service. This is required of the humblest, and no more is required of the noblest:

"He hath shewed thee, O man, what is good; and what doth the Lord require of thee, but to do justly, and to love mercy, and to walk humbly with thy God?"

VII

THE NATURE OF EVIL

Q. 7. How comes it that evil exists?

A. Evil is not an absolute thing, but has reference to a standard of attainment. The possibility of evil is the necessary consequence of a rise in the scale of moral existence; just as an organism whose normal temperature is far above "absolute zero" is necessarily liable to damaging and deadly cold. But cold is not in itself a positive or created thing.

CLAUSE VII

The term "evil" is relative: dirt, for instance, is well known to be only matter out of place; weeds are plants flourishing where they are not wanted; there are no weeds in botany, there are weeds in gardening; even disease is only one organism growing at the expense of another; ugliness is non-existent save to creatures with a sense of beauty, and is due to unsuitable grouping. Analysed into its elements, every particle of matter must be a miracle of law and order, and, in that sense, of beauty.

Recent discoveries in connexion with the internal structure of an atom, whereby the constituent particles are found to move in intricate and ascertainable orbits—leading to a new science of atomic astronomy—emphasise this assertion to an extent barely credible ten years ago.

Even what can be called filth—that is to say material which, to the casual observer, or when encountered at unsuitable times, is disgusting—may to an investigator, or under other circumstances, be of the highest interest; and may even arouse a sense of admiration, by reason of manifest subservience to function.

Many social evils are due to human folly and stupidity, and will cease when the race has risen to a standard already attained by individuals.

Excessive hunger and starvation are manifestly

evils of a negative character: they are merely a deficiency of supply: they have no business to exist in a civilised and organised community. Famine and pestilence can be checked by applications of science.

Pain is an awful reality, when highly developed organisms are subjected to wounds and poison and disease. Some kinds of pain have been wickedly inflicted by human beings on each other in the past, and other kinds may be removed or mitigated by the progress of discovery in the future. Physiologically the nerve processes involved are well worthy of study and control. Premature avoidance of pain would have been dangerous to the race, and not really helpful to the individual: but great advances in this direction are now foreshadowed. Already surgical operations can be conducted painlessly; and a time is foreshadowed when, through hypnosis, excessive and useless torture can be shut off from consciousness, by intelligence and will; somewhat as the random leakage of an electric supply can be checked. All this will come in due time:

> "The best is yet to be,
> The last of life for which the first was made:
> Our times are in His hand
> Who saith a whole I planned,
> Youth shows but half: trust God, see all, nor be afraid."

The contrast between good and evil can be well illustrated by the contrast between heat and cold.

Cold is only the absence of heat, and is made at once possible and necessary by the existence of degrees of heat. The fact that we regard excessive cold as an evil is only because our organisation demands a certain temperature for life; there is nothing evil about cold in itself: it is only evil in its relation to organisms sufficiently high to be damaged by it. The real *fact* is their normally high temperature, and their delicacy of response to stimuli. These things are good; and the only evil is a defect or deficiency of these good things.

Every rise involves the possibility of fall. Every advance seems to entail a corresponding penalty.

The power of assimilating food leaves the organism open to the pangs of hunger, that is, of insufficient nutriment,—manifestly only the absence of a good.

In a world devoid of life there is no death; in a world without conscious beings there is no sin. In a world without affection there would be no grief; and to a larger vision much of our grief may be needless:—

> "My son, the world is dark with griefs and graves,
> So dark that men cry out against the Heavens.
> Who knows but that the darkness is in man?"

A mechanical universe might be perfectly good. Every atom of matter perfectly obeys the forces acting upon it, and there is no error or wickedness or fault or rebellion in lifeless nature. Evil only begins when existence takes a higher turn. There is not even destruction or death in the inorganic world—only transformation. The higher possibility called life entails the correlative evils called death and disease. The possibility of keen sensation, which permits pleasure, also involves capacity for the corresponding penalty called pain: but the pain is in ourselves, and is the result of our sensitiveness combined with imperfection.

The still higher attribute of conscious striving after holiness, which must be the prerogative of free agents capable of virtue or purposed good, and marks so enormous a rise in the scale of creation,—involves the possibility that beings so endowed may fall from their high level, and, by definitely applying themselves to harm instead of good, may abuse their high power and suffer the penalty called sin; but the evil in all cases is a warped or distorted good, and has reference to the higher beings which are now in existence.

"There shall never be one lost good! what was shall live as before;
The evil is null, is nought, is silence implying sound;
What was good shall *be* good, with, for evil, so much good more;
On the earth the broken arcs; in the heaven a perfect round."

Some further idea of the necessity for evil can be conveyed as follows:—

Contrast is an inevitable attribute of reality. Sickness is the negative and opposite of health: without sickness we should not be aware what health was. There is no sickness in inorganic nature; yet, even there, contrast is the essence of existence. Everything that *is* must be surrounded by regions where it is not. There is no stupid infinity, or absence of boundaries, about existing things,—however infinite their totality may be,—no absence of limitation, either of perfection or of anything else. Existence involves limitation. A tree that is *here* is excluded from being everywhere else. Goodness would have no meaning if badness were impossible or non-existent.

> "No ill no good! such counter-terms, my son,
> Are border-races, holding, each its own
> By endless war."

We are not machines or automata, but free and conscious and active agents, and so must contend with evil as well as rejoice in good. Conflict and difficulty are essential for our training and development: even for our existence at this grade. With their aid we have become what we are; without them we should vegetate and degenerate; whereas the will of the Universe is that we arise and walk.

VIII

THE MEANING OF SIN

Q. 8. *What is sin?*

A. Sin is the deliberate and wilful act of a free agent who sees the better and chooses the worse, and thereby acts injuriously to himself and others. The root sin is selfishness, whereby needless trouble and pain are inflicted on others; when fully developed it involves moral suicide.

CLAUSE VIII

The essence of sin is error against light and knowledge, and against our own higher nature. Vice is error against natural law. Crime is error against society. Sin against our own higher nature may be truly said to be against God, because it is against that purpose or destiny which by Divine arrangement is open to us, if only we will pursue and realise it.

Sin is a disease: the whole of existence is so bound together that disease in one part means pain throughout; the innocent may suffer with the guilty, and suffering may extend to the Highest. The healing influences of forgiveness, felt by the broken and the contrite heart, achieve spiritual reform though they remove no penalty. Every eddy of conduct, for good or ill, must have its definite consequence.

We have high authority for the statement that hard circumstances and disabilities, not of our own making, are mercifully taken into account; while privileges and advantages weigh heavily in the scale against us, if we prove unworthy:

> "If ye were blind ye would have no sin;
> but now ye say We see, therefore your sin remaineth."

A man's or woman's nature may be so weakened and warped by miserable surroundings, that its strength is insufficient to cope with its environment. Pity, and a wish to help, are the feelings which such a state of things should arouse, together with an active determination to improve or remove the conditions which lead to such an untoward result. Most human failures are the result of bad social arrangements, and they constitute an indictment against human inertness and selfishness. It is a terrible responsibility to turn a human soul out of terrestrial life worse than when it entered that phase of existence. In so far as it accomplishes that, humanity is performing the function of a devil. Deterioration of others is usually achieved under the influence of some of the protean forms of social greed and selfishness.

Another reason why selfishness is spoken of as specially deadly, and even suicidal, depends upon certain regions of scientific inquiry not yet incorporated into orthodox science and therefore still to be regarded as speculative; it may be outlined as follows:—

Our present familiar methods of communicating with each other are such as speech, writing, and other conventional codes of signs more or less developed. It appears possible that a germ or nucleus of another, apparently immediate or directly psychical, method of communication may also exist; which has nothing to do with our known bodily organs, although its impressions are apprehended or interpreted by the receiver as if they were due to customary modes or forms of sensation. Whether that be so or not, it is certain that bodily neighbourhood and blood relationship confer opportunities for making friends which should be utilised to the utmost, and that friendship and affection are the most important things in life.

The intercourse with, and active assistance of, others

enlarges our own nature; and hereafter, when we have lost our bodily organs, it is probable that we shall be able to communicate only with those with whom we are connected by links of sympathy and affection.

A person who cuts himself off from all human intercourse and lives a miserly self-centred life, will ultimately, therefore, find himself alone in the universe; and, unless taken pity on and helped in a spirit of self-sacrifice, may as well be out of existence altogether. (A book called *Cecilia de Noel* emphasises this truth under the guise of a story.) That is why developed selfishness is spoken of as moral suicide: it is one of those evil things which truly assault and hurt the soul. It is a disintegrating and repelling agency. Love is the linking and uniting force in the spiritual universe, enabling it to cohere into a unity, in analogy with attractive forces in the material cosmos.

It has been necessary to dwell on the sin and pain and sorrow in the world, but the amount of good must be emphatically recognised too.

Our highest aspirations, and longings for something better, are a sign that better things exist. It is not given to the creature to exceed the Creator in imagination or in goodness; and the best and highest we can imagine shall be more than fulfilled by reality—in due time:—

> "All we have willed or hoped or dreamed of good, shall exist:
> Not its semblance, but itself; . . .
> When eternity affirms the conception of an hour."

IX

DEVELOPMENT OF LIFE

Q. 9. Are there beings lower in the scale of existence than man?

A. Yes, multitudes. In every part of the earth where life is possible, there we find it developed. Life exists in every variety of animal, in earth and air and sea, and in every species of plant.

CLAUSE IX

One of the facts of nature which we must weld into our conception of the scheme of the universe, is the strenuous effort made by all live things to persist in multifarious ways,—spreading out into quite unlikely regions, in the struggle for existence, and establishing themselves wherever life is possible. The fish slowly developing into a land animal, the reptile beginning to raise itself in the air and ultimately becoming a bird, the mammal returning under stress of circumstances to the water, as a seal or whale, or betaking itself to the air in search of food, in the form of a bat,—all these are instances of a universal tendency throughout animate nature.

Sometimes this determined effort at persistence breeds forms that appear to us ugly and deleterious. For the struggle results not only in beneficent organisms, but also in parasites and pests and blights, and may be held to account for the numerous cases of the interference of one form of life with another: one form utilising another for its own growth, and sometimes destroying that other in the process. It accounts also for the ravages of disease, which for the most part is an outcome of the establishment of a foreign and alien growth in a living body of higher grade,—a growth whose vital secretions are poisonous to its temporary host. On the other hand, the theory of manuring, the purification of rivers, the treatment of sewage, the use of opsonins and of serum-injections,—all illustrate the ministration of one form of life to another; they exhibit the contribution of beneficent organisms,—that is, of forms of life which promote higher development and conduce to well-being.

Many of the microbes and bacteria and low forms of cell life are beneficent in this way; and it is our function,—as ourselves one of the forms of life,—now consciously to intervene and take control of these vital processes. By investigation and study we can gradually understand the condition and life-history of each organism, and then can take such measures as will encourage the beneficent forms whether plant or animal, and destroy or eliminate those which from the human point of view are deadly and destructive,—attacking them at their weakest and most vulnerable stage. Widely regarded or interpreted, this function covers an immense range of possible activity—from every kind of scientific agriculture and the extirpating of tropical diseases, to the reformation of slum dwellings and the encouragement of physical training and school hygiene. As part of our work in regulating this planet and utilising its possibilities to the utmost for higher purposes, the regulation of vital conditions is probably our most pressing, and also at present our most neglected, corporate duty. Stupidity and a mistaken parsimony are among the serious obstacles with which the progressive portions of humanity have to contend.

Another aspect of the universal struggle for self-manifestation and corporeal realisation, which plays so large a part in all activity and is especially marked in the domain of life, is illustrated on a higher level by that overpowering instinct or impulse towards production and self-realisation, which is characteristic of genius. It may be said that throughout nature, from the lowest to the highest, a tendency to self-realisation, and a manifestation of joy in existence, are conspicuous.

It is thought that something akin to this tendency is exhibited in a region beyond and above what is ordinarily conceived of as "Nature." The process of evolution can be regarded as the gradual unfolding of the Divine Thought, or *Logos*, throughout the universe, by the action of Spirit upon matter. Achievement seems as if irradiated by a certain Happiness: and thus a poet like Browning is led to speak of the Divine Being as renewing his ancient creative rapture in the processes of nature:—joying in the sunbeams basking upon sand, sharing the pleasures of the wild life in the creatures of the woods,

> "Where dwells enjoyment there is He;"

and so to conjecture that

> "God tastes an infinite joy
> In infinite ways—one everlasting bliss
> From whom all being emanates, all power
> Proceeds; in whom is life for evermore."

X

COSMIC INTELLIGENCE

Q. 10. *Are there any beings higher in the scale of existence than man?*

A. Man is the highest of the dwellers on the planet earth, but the earth is only one of many planets warmed by the sun, and the sun is only one of a myriad of similar suns, which are so far off that we barely see them, and group them indiscriminately as "stars." We may reasonably conjecture that in some of the innumerable worlds circling round those distant suns there must be beings far higher in the scale of existence than ourselves; indeed, we have no knowledge which enables us to assert the absence of intelligence anywhere.

CLAUSE X

The existence of higher beings and of a Highest Being is a fundamental element in every religious creed. There is no scientific reason for imagining it possible that man is the highest intelligent existence—there is no reason to suppose that we dwellers on this planet know more about the universe than any other existing creature. Such an idea, strictly speaking, is absurd. Science has investigated our ancestry and shown that we are the product of planetary processes. We may be, and surely must be, something more, but this we clearly are—a development of life on this planet earth. Science has also revealed to us an innumerable host of other worlds, and has relegated the earth to its now recognised subordinate place as one of a countless multitude of worlds.

Consider a spherical region bounded by the distance of the farthermost stars visible in the strongest telescope, or say with a radius corresponding to a parallax of one-thousandth of a second of arc, so that the time taken by light to travel right across it is 6000 years:—Lord Kelvin, treating of such a portion of Universe, says:

"There may also be a large amount of matter in many stars outside the sphere of 3.10^{16} kilometres radius, but however much matter there may be outside it, it seems to be made highly probable, by

§§ 11–21, that the total quantity of matter within it is greater than 100 million times, and less than 2000 million times, the sun's mass" (*Philosophical Magazine*, August 1901).

It does not follow that all this matter is distributed in masses like our sun with its attendant planets; but, on the average, that is as likely an arrangement as another, and it corresponds with what we know.

So, given, on this hypothesis, the existence of some thousand million solar systems or families of worlds, within our ken, and knowing what we do about the exuberant impulse towards vital development wherever it is possible, we must conclude that those worlds contain life; and if so, it is against all reasonable probability that the only world of which we happen to know the details contains the creature highest in the entire scale. It would be just as reasonable to imagine, what we happen to know is false, that our particular sun is the largest, and our particular planet the brightest of all, as it is to conjecture that this world is the highest and best, or the only one in existence.

The self-glorifying instinct of the human mind has resented this negative conclusion, and for long clung to the Ptolemaic idea that the earth was no mere planet among a crowd of others, but was the centre of the universe; and that the sun and all the stars were subsidiary to it. A Ptolemaic idea clings to some of us still—not now as regards the planet, but as regards man; and we, insignificant creatures, with senses only just open to the portentous meaning of the starry sky, presume—some of us—to deny the existence of higher powers and higher knowledge than our own. We are accustomed to be careful as to what we assert; we are liable to be unscrupulous as to what we deny. It is possible to find people who, knowing nothing or next to nothing of the Universe, are prepared to limit existence to that of which they have had experience, and to measure the cosmos in terms of their own understanding. Their confidence in themselves, their shut minds and self-satisfied hearts, are things to marvel at. The fact is that no glimmer of a conception of the real magnitude and complexity of existence can ever have illuminated their cosmic view.

XI

IMMANENCE

Q. 11. *What caused and what maintains existence?*

A. Of our own knowledge we are unable to realise the meaning of origination or of maintenance; all that we ourselves can accomplish in the physical world is to move things into desired positions, and leave them to act on each other. Nevertheless our effective movements are all inspired by thought, and so we conceive that there must be some Intelligence immanent in all the processes of nature, for they are not random or purposeless, but organised and beautiful.

CLAUSE XI

ORIGIN

We cannot conceive the origin of any fundamental existence. We can describe the beginning of any particular object in its present shape, but its substance always existed in some other shape previously; and nothing really either springs into being or ceases to exist. A cloud or dew becomes visible, and then evaporates, seeming to spring into being and then vanish away; but as water vapour it had a past history and will have a future, both apparently without limit. In our own case, and in the case of any live thing, the history is unknown to us; but ultimate origin or absolute beginning, save of individual collocations, is unthinkable.

The truth that science teaches, on the one hand, is that everything is a perpetual flux,

πάντα ῥεῖ καὶ οὐδὲν μένει,

that nothing is permanent and fixed and unchangeable:

> "The hills are shadows, and they flow
> From form to form, and nothing stands;
> They melt like mists, the solid lands,
> Like clouds they shape themselves and go."

On the other hand, we learn that, in its ultimate essence and reality, everything is persistent and eternal; that it is the form alone that changes, while the substance endures. No end and no beginning—a continual Eternal Now—this is the scientific interpretation of I AM.

There are those who think that in the last resort the ultimate reality will be found to be of the nature of Spirit, Consciousness, and Mind. It may be so—it probably is so—but that is a teaching of Philosophy, not at present of Science.

The teaching of religion may be summarised thus:

"All that exists, exists only by the communication of God's infinite being. All that has intelligence, has it only by derivation from His sovereign reason; and all that acts, acts only from the impulse of His supreme activity. It is He who does all in all; it is He who, at each instant of our life, is the beating of our heart, the movement of our limbs, the light of our eyes, the intelligence of our spirit, the soul of our soul."—*Fénelon.*

MAINTENANCE

So also with regard to maintenance.

The multifarious processes around us—the succession of the seasons, the flow of sap in trees, the circulation of our own blood, the digestion of our food—all these things are beyond our power, and are not contrived or managed by our conscious agency—not even the occurrences in our own bodies. But by means of such unconscious processes our muscular and nervous systems are supplied with nutriment, and we thus become master of a certain amount of energy.

The energy of our muscles, or of some of them, is within our control, and we can thereby direct other physical energies into desired channels; but we cannot in the slightest degree alter the amount of that energy. We utilise terrestrial energy, by directing and controlling its transformations and transferences, within the limits of our knowledge; but we do it always by moving material objects, and in no other way. For instance, we cannot directly or consciously generate an electric current, or magnetism, or light, or life; for all these things we depend upon partially explored properties of matter, which we can arrange in a certain way so as to achieve a desired end.

A multitude of complex processes are constantly occurring in our bodies without any intervention of consciousness; and though we may make a study of the functions of the several organs, and gradually learn something about them, it is a study as of something outside ourselves; the due performance of bodily function is independent of our volition. We can interfere with and damage our organs, and with skill we can so arrange damaged parts that the self-healing process shall have time and opportunity to act; we can also introduce beneficent agencies and stimulating drugs; but our power of direct action is practically limited to muscular and mental activity.

Digression on Rudimentary Physiology

It is well for children to have some conception of the complex processes constantly occurring in their own organisms.

The fact that the heart is a continuously acting pump, urging the blood along arteries to the tissues,—to places where it picks up nutriment, to places where the crudely enriched blood is oxidised, to places where the elaborated material is deposited so as to replenish waste and effect growth—all this should be known; and the partial analogy with the sap of trees, rising in the trunk to be elaborated in the leaves by means of sunshine and air, and then descending ready to be deposited as liquid wood, can be pointed out.

The function of the lungs, wherein the blood dispersed throughout a spongy texture is exposed in immense surface to the air, without loss or leakage other than what properly transpires through the membranes, and the consequent advantage of deep breathing and of fresh clean air,—all this has a practical as well as a theoretical interest.

The lungs are more under voluntary control than the heart, but the way exercise increases the circulation, and generally blows the fires of the body, is also of practical interest.

Some idea of the processes of digestion can be given, especially the function of the stomach and the intestines; the liver may be too difficult, but the salivary glands are fairly simple, and so are the kidneys and the skin. The way the muscles act as an efficient mechanical engine, depending on the consumption of fuel and the conservation of energy, can be superficially explained, with some idea of the stimulating nervous system and controlling brain cells. The sensory nerves and specialised nerve-endings demand specific treatment.

These and other physiological details may seem out of place, but they are strictly appropriate; for the essence of Immanence is that nothing is common or unclean, until abused: and the nobler the faculty, the fouler is the degradation caused by its abuse. A sense of the responsibility involved in the possession or lease of all this intricate mass of mechanism, intrusted to our care, and the wish to keep it in good order—without giving unnecessary trouble to others to set it right, and without blaspheming the Maker by applying it to bad and ignoble ends—will arise almost imperceptibly, when the body is even begun to be understood. Many faults originate in ignorance and want of thought.

Mind and Matter

Among the material objects we move are the parts of our own bodies; indeed, it is through muscular intervention or agency that we act on bodies in general. We know of no other method. Even when we *speak* we are only moving certain face and throat and chest muscles, so as to generate condensations and rarefactions in the air; which, travelling by dynamical properties, excite corresponding vibrations or movements in the ear drum of our auditor;—vibrations not in themselves intelligible, but demanding interpretation from the recipient. So also it is with the traces of ink left on paper by our muscular action when we write. Only to a perceptive eye, and informed and kindred mind, have they any meaning.

It is probable that even when we think, some special atomic motion goes on in the brain cells, though this is an example of *unconscious* movement, of which there are many examples in bodily function; but directly we begin to attend to mental processes we leave the physical region as understood by us, and enter a more deeply mysterious psychical region. Unknown as this is for purposes of analysis, from the point of view of experience it is more immediately familiar than any other; since it is through the activity of mind that every other kind of existence is necessarily inferred. Thought is our mechanism or instrument of knowledge—through it we know everything—but thought is not what we directly know. Primarily we think of *things*, not of thought itself. So also sight is our instrument of seeing—through light we see—but it is not light that we perceive, rather it is the objects which send it in certain patterns to our eyes.

Whereas we can act on the external world only through our muscles; in ourselves we are aware of things belonging to a totally different category, with which muscle and movement and energy appear to have nothing to do,—such things as thought, purpose, desire, humour, affection, consciousness, will. These mental faculties seem intimately associated with, and are displayed by, our bodily mechanism; but in themselves they belong to a different order of being,—an order which employs and dominates the material, while immersed or immanent in it. Every purposed movement is preceded and inspired by thought.

Such reasoned control, by indwelling mind, may be undetectable and inconceivable to a low order of intelligence, being totally masked by the material garment; and the purpose underlying our activity may have to be inferred, by such intelligence, with as great difficulty as we feel in detecting indwelling Purpose amid the spontaneous operations of Nature.

Nevertheless, whenever our movements are not controlled by thought and intelligent purpose, but are left to chance and random impulses, like the actions of a man whose reason has been unseated, nothing but error and confusion results;—quite a different state of things from anything we observe in the orderly and beautiful procedure of nature.

It is sometimes said that the operations of nature are spontaneous; and that is exactly what they are. That is the meaning of immanence. "Spontaneous," used in this sense, does not mean random and purposeless and undetermined: it means actuated and controlled from within, by something indwelling and all pervading and not absent anywhere. The intelligence which guides things is not something external to the scheme, clumsily interfering with it by muscular action, as we are constrained to do when we interfere at all; but is something within and inseparable from it, as human thought is within and inseparable from the action of our brains.

In some partially similar way we conceive that the multifarious processes in nature, with neither the origin nor maintenance of which have we had anything to do, must be guided and controlled by some Thought and Purpose, immanent in everything, but revealed only to those with sufficiently awakened perceptions. Many are blind to the meaning—to the fact even that there is a meaning—in nature; just as an animal is usually blind to a picture, and always to a poem; but to the higher members of our race the Intelligence and Purpose, underlying the whole mystery of existence, elaborating the details of evolution—and ultimately tending to elucidate the frequent discords, the strange humours, and puzzling contradictions of life—are keenly felt. To them the lavish beauty of wild Nature—of landscape, of sunset, of mountain, and of sea—are revelations of an indwelling Presence, rejoicing in its own majestic order.

πάντα πλήρη θεῶν.

"Earth's crammed with Heaven
And every common bush afire with God."

The idea that the world as we know it arose by chance and fortuitous concourse of atoms is one that no science really sustains, though such an idea is the superficial outcome of an incipient recognition of the uniformity of nature—a sequel to the perception that there is no capricious or spasmodic interference with the course of events, and no changes of purpose observable therein, such as we are accustomed to in works of human ingenuity and skill. We are accustomed to associate "will" with the degenerate form of it called caprice, and to consider that "purpose" must be accompanied by changes of purpose; so that a steady, uniform, persistent course of action is puzzling to us, and wears the superficial aspect of mechanism. An omnipresent, uniform, immanent Purpose, running through the whole of existence without break of continuity or change of aim, is beyond our experience; and, like every other uniformity, is difficult to detect or realise. As an instance of this difficulty, I need only cite the long-delayed discovery of an all-embracing medium like the terrestrial atmosphere. An intelligent deep-sea creature would find it most difficult to become aware of the existence of water. Similarly humanity has existed all along in a pervading and interpenetrating ether, of which to this day men have for the most part no cognisance; although it is probably the fundamental substratum of the whole material world, underlying every kind of activity, and constituting the very atoms of which their own bodies are composed.

Looking at the truths of geometry, the laws of nature, and the beauty and organisation of the visible world, it is as impossible rationally to suppose that they arose by chance, or by mere contentious jostling, as it is to suppose that a work of literature or a piece of music was composed in that way.

The process of evolution appears to us self-sustained and self-guided, because the guidance is uniform and constant.

In nature, heredity and survival will explain the persistence of a favourable variation when once originated, but the origin of variations is still mysterious, and the full meaning of heredity is not yet unravelled.

The struggle for existence has been one of the means whereby animal life has been developed and perfected; but now that it has become conscious and purposeful, in humanity, the apparently blind struggle is suspended at the higher level, and the weak and suffering are attended to and helped—not exterminated. There must always be disciplinary effort: but it can be effort for something better than bare subsistence; it can conduce to evolution of character, and development of soul. Mere struggle and survival is an inferior instrument of progress, and it can be superseded wherever it has done its necessary preliminary work. The Divine purpose is fulfilled in many ways; and far more can be expected of self-conscious evolution than of the long slow process which has rendered it possible.

The kind of selection actually or best known to us is that which has been directed by human beings; and inasmuch as the highest human beings are themselves conscious of help and guidance, it is to be assumed that such help and guidance has been in constant activity all along, operating on, or rather in, the refractory materials, so as slowly to develop in them the power of manifesting not only life and beauty, but also consciousness, spiritual perception, and free will.

XII

SOUL AND SPIRIT

Q. 12. What is to be said of man's higher faculties?

A. The faculties and achievements of the highest among mankind—in Art, in Science, in Philosophy, and in Religion—are not explicable as an outcome of a struggle for existence. Something more than mere life is possessed by us—something represented by the words "mind" and "soul" and "spirit." On one side we are members of the animal kingdom; on another we are associates in a loftier type of existence, and are linked with the Divine.

CLAUSE XII

The highest of those who have walked the earth reveal to us what we, too, may some day be: they link us with the Divine, and teach us that, however pathetically defaced by our infirmities and distorted by our imperfections, we may yet reflect the image of God.

[*Part of the following explanation is based upon a study of certain facts not yet fully incorporated into orthodox science, nor fully recognised by philosophy: it must therefore be regarded as speculation.*]

This idea, which permeates literature—that man has a spiritual as well as a material origin—emphasises from another point of view the doctrine of the Fall. For the utilisation of a material body, of animal ancestry, exposes the individual to much trial and temptation, and makes him aware of a contest between the flesh and the spirit, or between a lower and a higher self, which constitutes the element of truth in the otherwise mistaken doctrine of "original," or inherited, or imputed sin. Vicarious sin is a legal fiction: so is vicarious punishment; vicarious suffering is a reality. The mother of a ne'er-do-well knows it: it is undergone by the children of vicious parents; the highest souls have felt it on behalf of the race of man; but it is not artificial or imputed suffering, it is genuine and real; and experience shows that it can have a redeeming virtue.

The double nature of man,—the inherited animal tendencies, and the inspired spiritual aspirations, if they can both be fully admitted, reconcile many difficulties. Our body is an individual collocation of cells, which began to form and grow together at a certain date, and will presently be dispersed; but the constructing and dominating reality, called our "soul," did not then begin to exist; nor will it cease with bodily decay. Interaction with the material world then began, and will then cease, but we ourselves in essence are persistent and immortal. Even our personality and individuality may be persistent, if our character be sufficiently developed to possess a reality of its own. In our present state, truly, the memory of our past is imperfect or non-existent; but when we waken and shake off the tenement of matter, our memory and consciousness may enlarge too, as we rejoin the larger self of which only a part is now manifested in mortal flesh.

The ancient doctrine of a previous state of existence, of which we are now entranced into forgetfulness, is inculcated in the familiar lines—

> "Our birth is but a sleep and a forgetting;
> The Soul that rises with us, our life's star,
> Hath had elsewhere its setting,
> And cometh from afar:
> Not in entire forgetfulness,
> And not in utter nakedness,
> But trailing clouds of glory do we come
> From God, who is our home,"

the idea being that the forgetfulness is not complete, especially during infancy; nor need it be complete in moments of inspiration. Myers' doctrine of the subliminal self is an expanded and modified form of this idea, and is to a large extent apparently justified by a certain range of psychological inquiry: though Myers lays stress, not on memory of a past, but on a present occasional intercommunication between the part and the whole.

The Platonic doctrine of reminiscence exnibits one variety of the idea of pre-existence, though in a necessarily inaccurate and somewhat fanciful form—as though infants were a stage higher in the scale than grown men. Such an idea would involve the old mistaken postulate of initial perfection, which was made long ago concerning the race: whereas the truth was innocency, not perfection. But the idea that nothing less than the whole of a personality must be incarnated—even in the body of an infant—leads to innumerable difficulties;—it does not even escape unanswerable questions about trivialities such as the moment of arrival; and it is responsible for much biological scepticism concerning the existence of any soul at all. Whereas, on the strength of the experience that all processes in nature are really gradual, the idea of gradual incarnation—increasing as the brain and body grow, but never attaining any approach to completeness even in the greatest of men—sets one above innumerable petty difficulties, and to me seems an opening in the direction of the truth. On this view, the portion of larger self incarnated in an infant or a feeble-minded person is but small: in normal cases, more appears as the body is fitted to receive it. In some cases much appears, thus constituting a great man; while in others, again, a link of occasional communication is left open between the part and the whole—producing what we call "genius." Second childishness is the gradual abandonment of the material vehicle, as it gets worn out or damaged. But, during the episode of this life, man is never a complete self, his roots are in another order of being, he is moving about in worlds not realised, he is as if walking in a vain shadow and disquieting himself in vain.

It may be objected that our present existence is very far from being a dream or trance-like condition, that we are very wide awake to the "realities" of the world, and very keen about "things of importance"; that an analogy drawn from the memories of hypnotic patients and multiple personalities, and other pathological cases, is sure to be misleading. It may be so, the idea is admittedly of the nature of speculation; but the greatest of poets lends his countenance to the notion that phenomena and appearances are not ultimate realities, that our present life is not unlike the state of a sleep-walker—that we slept to enter it, and must sleep again before we wake—

"We are such stuff
As dreams are made of, and our little life
Is rounded with a sleep."

As to the question whether we ever again live on earth, it appears unlikely on this view that a given developed individual will appear again in unmodified form. If my present self is a fraction of a larger self, some other fraction of that larger self may readily be thought of as appearing,—to gain practical experience in the world of matter, and to return with developed character to the whole whence it sprang. And this operation may be repeated frequently; but these hypothetical fractional appearances can hardly be spoken of as reincarnations. We must not dogmatise, however, on the subject, and the case of the multitudes at present thwarted and returned at infancy may demand separate treatment. It may be that the abortive attempts at development on the part of individuals are like the waves lapping up the sides of a boulder and being successively flung back; while the general advance of the race is typified by the steady rising of the tide.

Soul and Body

The philosophic doctrine of the "self" on this view is a difficult one, and involves much study. As here stated, the form is sure to be crude and imperfect. Philosophy resents any sharp distinction between soul and body, between indwelling self and material vehicle. It prefers to treat the self as a whole, an individual unit; though it may admit the actual agglomeration of material particles to be transient and temporary. The word "self" can be used in a narrower or in a broader sense. It may signify the actual continuity of personality and memory whereof we are conscious; or it may signify a larger and vaguer underlying reality, of which the conscious self is but a fraction. The narrower sense is wide enough to include the whole man, both soul and body, as we know him; but the phrase "subliminal self" covers ideas extending hypothetically beyond that.

The idea of Redemption or Regeneration, in its highest and most Christian form, is applicable to both soul and body. The life of Christ shows us that the whole man can be regenerated as he stands; that we have not to wait for a future state, that the Kingdom of Heaven is in our midst and may be assimilated by us here and now.

The term "salvation" should not be limited to the soul, but should apply to the whole man. What kind of transfiguration may be possible, *or may have been possible*, in the case of a perfectly emancipated and glorified body, we do not yet know.

In a still larger sense these terms apply to the whole race of man; and for the salvation of mankind individual loss and suffering have been gladly expended. Not the individual alone, but the race also, can be adjured to realise some worthy object for all its striving, to open its eyes to more glorious possibilities than it has yet perceived, to

> ". . . climb the Mount of Blessing, whence, if thou
> Look higher, then—perchance—thou mayest—beyond
> A hundred ever-rising mountain lines,
> And past the range of Night and Shadow—see
> The high-heaven dawn of more than mortal day
> Strike on the Mount of Vision!"

XIII

GRACE

Q. 13. *Is man helped in his struggle upward?*

A. There is a Power in the Universe vastly beyond our comprehension; and we trust and believe that it is a Good and Loving Power, able and willing to help us and all creatures, and to guide us wisely, without detriment to our incipient freedom. This Loving-kindness continually surrounds us; in it we live and have our real being; it is the mainspring of joy and love and beauty, and we call it the Grace of God. It sustains and enriches all worlds, and may take a multiplicity of forms, but it was specially manifested to dwellers on this planet in the life of Jesus Christ, through whose spirit and living influence the race of man may hope to rise to heights at present inaccessible.

CLAUSE XIII

The guidance exercised by the Divine Spirit, by which we are completely surrounded, is not of the nature of compulsion ; it is only a leading and helping influence, which we are able to resist if we choose.

The problem of manufacturing free creatures with a will of their own, to be led, not forced, into right action, is a problem of a different nature from any of those that have ever appealed to human power and knowledge. What we are accustomed to make is mechanism, of various kinds; and the essential difficulty of the higher problem is so obscure to us that some impatient and unimaginative persons cry out against its slowness, and wonder that everything is not compulsorily made perfect at once. But we can see that the kind of perfection thus easily attainable would be of an utterly inferior kind.

It is to be supposed that incarnation, or a connexion between consciousness and material mechanism, is auxiliary to the difficult process of evolution of free beings, thus indicated; and it is probable that matter is thus an instrument of lofty spiritual purpose. Some religious systems have failed to perceive this, and have depreciated matter and flesh as intrinsically evil.

One important feature of Christianity is that it recognises as good the connexion between spirit and matter, and emphasises the importance of both, when properly regarded. It is not mystical and spiritual alone, nor is it material alone; but it tends to unify these two extremes, and to place in due position both soul and body: the material being utilised to make manifest the spiritual, and being dominated by it.

The whole idea of the Incarnation, as well as some of the miracles and the sacraments, are expressive of this wide and comprehensive character of the Christian religion.

It recognises the wonder and beauty of the animal body, destined to be the scene of extraordinary spiritual triumphs in the long course of time; and it teaches

> "That none but Gods could build this house of ours,
> So beautiful, vast, various, so beyond
> All work of man, yet, like all work of man,
> A beauty with defect—till That which knows,
> And is not known, but felt thro' what we feel
> Within ourselves is highest, shall descend
> On this half-deed, and shape it at the last
> According to the Highest in the Highest."

Christianity is a planetary and human religion: being the revelation of those aspects of Godhead which are most intelligible and helpful to us in our present stage of development. But it is more than a revelation, it is a manifestation of some of the attributes of Godhead in the form of humanity.

The statement that Christ and God are one, is not really a statement concerning Christ, but a statement concerning what we understand by God. It is useless, and in the literal sense preposterous, to explain the known in terms of the unknown: the converse is the right method. "He that hath seen me hath seen the Father." Every son of man is potentially also a son of God, but the union was deepest and completest in the Galilean.

The ideas of incarnation and revelation are not confined to the domain of religion; they are common to music and letters and science: in all we recognise "a flash of the will that can,"

> "All through my keys that gave their sounds to a wish of my soul,
> All through my soul that praised, as the wish flowed visibly forth."

The spirit of Beethoven is incarnate in his music; and he that hath heard the Fifth Symphony hath heard Beethoven.

The Incarnation of the Divine Spirit in man is the central feature of Terrestrial History. It is through man, and the highest man, that the revelation of what is meant by Godhead must necessarily come. The world — even the common everyday world — has accepted this, and is able to perceive its appropriateness and truth; and the traditional song of the angels, at the epoch of the Birth—

> "Glory to God in the highest; and on earth peace, goodwill among men,"

is still heard in the land. Whenever there is war at Christmas-time it is universally felt to be incongruous.

Goodwill among men is conspicuous in cessation of private feuds, in overladen postbags, in family reunions and Christmas hampers and all manner of homely frivolities.

The Incarnation doctrine is the glorification of human effort, and the sanctification of childhood and simplicity of life; but it is a pity to reduce it to a dogma. It is well to leave something to intuitive apprehension, and to let the life and death of Christ gradually teach their own eloquent lesson without premature dogmatic assistance.

From that event we date our history, and the strongest believer in immanent Godhead can admit that the life of Jesus was an explicit and clear-voiced message of love to this planet from the Father of all. Naturally our conception of Godhead is still only indistinct and partial, but, so far as we are as yet able to grasp it, we must reach it through recognition of the extent and intricacy of the Cosmos, and more particularly through the highest type and loftiest spiritual development of man himself.

The most essential element in Christianity is its conception of a human God; of a God, in the first place, not apart from the Universe, not outside it and distinct from it, but immanent in it; yet not immanent only, but actually incarnate, incarnate in it and revealed in the Incarnation. The nature of God is displayed in part by everything, to those who have eyes to see, but is displayed most clearly and fully by the highest type of existence, the highest experience to which the process of evolution has so far opened our senses.

> "'Tis the sublime of man,
> Our noontide majesty, to know ourselves
> Part and proportion of one wondrous whole."

The Humanity of God, the Divinity of man, is the essence of the Christian revelation. It was truly a manifestation of Immanuel.

The Christian idea of God is not that of a being outside the universe, above its struggles and advances, looking on and taking no part in the process, *solely* exalted, beneficent, self-determined, and complete. It is also that of a God who loves, who yearns, who suffers, who keenly laments the rebellious and misguided activity of the free agents brought into being by Himself as part of Himself, who enters into the storm and conflict, and is subject to conditions as the soul of it all.

This is the truth which has been reverberating down the ages ever since; it has been the hidden inspiration of saint, apostle, prophet, martyr, and, in however dim and vague a form, has given hope and consolation to the unlettered and poverty-stricken millions:—A God that could understand, that could suffer, that could sympathise, that had felt the extremity of human anguish, the agony of bereavement, had submitted even to the brutal hopeless torture of the innocent, and had become acquainted with the pangs of death—this has been the chief consolation of the Christian religion. This is the extraordinary conception of Godhead to which we have thus far risen. "This is My beloved Son."

"Enough that he heard it once; we shall hear it by and by." The Christian God is revealed as the incarnate Spirit of humanity; or rather the incarnate spirit of humanity is recognised as a real intrinsic part of God. "The Kingdom of Heaven is within you."

XIV

INSPIRATION

Q. 14. *How may we become informed concerning things too high for our own knowledge?*

A. We should strive to learn from the great teachers, the prophets and poets and saints of the human race, and should seek to know and to interpret their inspired writings.

CLAUSE XIV

People at a low stage of development are liable to think that they can arrive at truth by their unaided judgment and insight, and that they need not concern themselves with the thoughts and experiences of the past. Unconscious of any inspiration themselves, they decline to believe in the possibility of such a thing, and regard it as a fanciful notion of unpractical and dreamy people.

Great men, on the other hand, are the fingerposts and lodestars of humanity; it is with their aid that we steer our course, if we are wise, and the records of their thought and inspiration are of the utmost value to us.

This is the meaning of literature in general, and of that mass of ancient religious literature in particular, on which hundreds of scholars have bestowed their best energies: now translated, bound together, and handed down to us as the Canon of Scripture, of which some portions are the most inspired writings yet achieved by humanity. It is impossible for us to ignore the concurrent mass of human testimony therein recorded, the substantial and general truth of which has been vouched for by the prophets and poets and seers of all time. Accordingly, if we are to form worthy beliefs regarding the highest conceptions in the Universe, we must avail ourselves of all this testimony; discriminating and estimating its relative value in the light of our own judgment and experience, studying such works and criticism as are accessible to us, asking for the guidance of the Divine Spirit, and seeking with modest and careful patience to apprehend something in the direction of the truth.

XV

A CREED

Q. 15. *What, then, do you reverently believe can be deduced from a study of the records and traditions of the past in the light of the present?*

A. I believe in one Infinite and Eternal Being, a guiding and loving Father, in whom all things consist.

I believe that the Divine Nature is specially revealed to man through Jesus Christ our Lord, who lived and taught and suffered in Palestine 1900 years ago, and has since been worshipped by the Christian Church as the immortal Son of God, the Saviour of the world.

I believe that the Holy Spirit is ever ready to help us along the Way towards Goodness and Truth; that prayer is a means of communion between man and God; and that it is our privilege through faithful service to enter into the Life Eternal, the Communion of Saints, and the Peace of God.

CLAUSE XV

Notes on the Creed

The three paragraphs correspond to the three aspects or Personifications of Deity which have most impressed mankind,—

The Creating and Sustaining.

The Sympathising and Suffering.

The Regenerating and Sanctifying.

The first of the three clauses tries to indicate briefly the cosmic, as well as the more humanly intelligible, attributes of Deity; and to suggest an idea of creation appropriate to the doctrine of Divine Immanence, as opposed to the anthropomorphic notion of manufacture. The idea of evolution by guiding and controlling Purpose is suggested, as well as the vital conception of Fatherly Love.

In the second paragraph, Time and Place are explicitly mentioned in order to emphasise the historical and human aspect of the Christian manifestation of Godhead. This aspect is essential and easy to appreciate, though its idealisation and full interpretation are difficult. The step, from the bare historic facts to the idealisation of the Fourth Gospel, has been the work of the Church, in the best sense of that word, aided by the doctrines of the Logos and of Immanence, elaborated by Philosophy. It all hangs together, when properly grasped, and constitutes a luminous conception; but the light thus shed upon the nature of Deity must not blind our eyes to the simple human facts from which it originally emanated. The clear and undoubted fact is that the founder of the Christian religion lived on this earth a blameless life, taught and helped the poor who heard him gladly, gathered to himself a body of disciples with whom he left a message to mankind, and was put to death as a criminal blasphemer, at the instigation of mistaken priests in the defence of their own Order and privileges.

This monstrous wrong is regarded by some as having unconsciously completed the salvation of the race; because of the consummation of sacrifice, and because of the suffering of the innocent, which it involved. The Jewish sacrificial system, and the priestly ceremony of the scapegoat, seem to lead up to that idea; which was elaborated by St. Paul with immense genius, and taught by S. Augustine.

Others attach more saving efficacy to the life, the example, and the teachings, as recorded in the Gospels; and all agree that they are important.

But in fact the whole is important: and at the foot of the Cross there has been a perennial experience of relief and renovation. Sin being the sense of imperfection, disunion, lack of harmony, the struggle among the members that St. Paul for all time expressed;—there is usually associated with it a sense of impotence, a recognition of the impossibility of achieving peace and unity in one's own person, a feeling that aid must be forthcoming from a higher source. It is this feeling which enables the spectacle of any noble self-sacrificing human action to have an elevating effect, it is this which gropes after the possibilities of the highest in human nature, it is a feeling which for large tracts of this planet has found its highest stimulus and completest satisfaction in the life and death of Christ.

The willingness of such a Being to share our nature, to live the life of a peasant, and to face the horrible certainty of execution by torture, in order personally to help those whom he was pleased to call his brethren, is a race-asset which, however masked and overlaid with foreign growths, yet gleams through every covering and suffuses the details of common life with fragrance.

This conspicuously has been a redeeming, or rather a regenerating, agency;—for by filling the soul with love and adoration and fellow-feeling for the Highest, the old cravings have often been almost hypnotically rendered distasteful and repellent, the bondage of sin has been loosened from many a spirit, the lower entangled self has been helped from the slough of despond and raised to the shores of a larger hope, whence it can gradually attain to harmony and peace.

The invitation to the troubled soul—"Come, and find rest"—has reference, not to relief from sin alone, but to all restlessness and lack of trust. The Atonement removes the feeling of dislocation ; it induces a tranquil sense of security and harmony,—an assurance of union with the Divine will.

Every form of Christianity aims at salvation for the race and for each individual, both soul and body; but different versions differ as to the means most efficient to this end. Varieties of Christianity can be grouped under the symbolic names, Paul, James, Peter, and John; with the dominating ideas of vicarious sacrifice, human effort, Church ordinance, and loving-kindness, respectively.

In the coldest system of nomenclature these four chief varieties may be styled, *legal*, *ethical*, *ecclesiastical*, and *emotional*, respectively. More favourably regarded, the dominating ideas may be classified thus:—

1. Faith in a divine scheme of redemption.
2. Simple life, social service, honesty, and virtue.
3. Spiritual sustenance by utilisation of means of grace.
4. Obedience, unworldliness, trust, and love.

With the treatment of these great themes, sectarian differences begin: differences which seem beyond our power to reconcile. We need not dwell on the differences, we would rather emphasise the mass of agreement. Probably there is an element of truth in every view that has long been held and found helpful by human beings, however overlaid with superstition it may in some cases have become ; and probably also the truth is far from exhausted by any one estimate of the essential feature of a Life which most of us can agree to recognise as a revelation of the high-water-mark of manhood, and a manifestation of the human attributes of God.

None of the above partially overlapping subdivisions of Christianity equals in importance the over-shadowing and dominating theory emphasised in the above creed: namely, the idea of a veritable incarnation of Divine Spirit—a visible manifestation of Deity immanent in humanity. The facts of the life, testified to by witnesses and idealised by philosophers and saints, have been transmitted down the centuries by a continuous Church; though with a mingling of superstition and error.

At present the process of interpretation has been accompanied by a sad amount of discord and hostility, to the scandal of the Church; but the future of religion shall not always be endangered by suspicion and intolerance and narrowness among professed disciples of truth. There must come a time when first a nation, and afterwards the civilised world, shall awake and glory in the light of the risen sun:—

> "—A sun but dimly seen
> Here, till the mortal morning mists of earth
> Fade in the noon of heaven, when creed and race
> Shall bear false witness, each of each, no more,
> But find their limits by that larger light,
> And overstep them, moving easily
> Thro' after-ages in the love of Truth,
> The truth of Love."

The emphasis laid by the above explanation on the conception of the human nature incorporated into Godhead, is appropriate to this country and to the Western World generally; but we thereby imply no abuse of the religions of the East, in their proper place, any more than of the religions of other planets. Silence concerning them is not disrespectful. It is not to be supposed that any one world has a monopoly of the Grace of God; nor does it exhaust every plan of salvation. In estimating the value ot another dispensation, or of any ill-understood religion (and no one can perfectly understand and appreciate more than one religion, if that, to the full), the old test is the only valid one: Do men gather grapes of thorns or figs of thistles?

The third paragraph speaks of our progress along the Way of Truth to goodness and beauty of Life, and of the assistance constantly vouchsafed to our own efforts in that direction. It is not by our own efforts alone that we can succeed, for we cannot tell what lies before us, and we lack wisdom to foresee the consequences of alternative courses of action,—one of which nevertheless we instinctively feel to be right. Acts of self-will, and fanatical determination, and impatience, may operate in the wrong direction altogether; and effort so expended may be worse than wasted. But if we submit ourselves wholly to a beneficent Power, and seek not our own ends but the ends of the Guiding Spirit of all things, we shall obtain peace in ourselves, and may hope to be used for purposes beyond what we can ask or think. This kind of service is what, in its several degrees, will be recognised by the Master as "faithful"; and it is by being faithful in a few things that hereafter we shall be found worthy of many things, and shall enter into the joy of our Lord.

By the Holy Spirit is meant the living and immanent Deity at work in the consciousness and experience of mankind,—the guider of human history, the comforter of human sorrow, the revealer of truth, the inspirer of faith and hope and love, the producer of life and joy and beauty, the sustainer and enricher of existence, the Impersonation of the Grace of God.

This mighty theme has been treated, in an initial manner, in connexion with Clause XIII.

Supplementary questions will be asked concerning other terms in the third paragraph; but as to the phrase with which the Creed concludes—the Peace of God,—its meaning, we are well assured, surpasses understanding, and can be felt only by experience; hence no supplementary question is asked concerning that phrase.

XVI

THE LIFE ETERNAL

Q. 16. *What do you mean by the Life Eternal?*

A. I mean that, whereas our terrestrial existence is temporary, our real existence continues without ceasing, in either a higher or a lower form, according to our use of opportunities and means of grace; and that the fulness of Life ultimately attainable represents a growing perfection at present inconceivable by us.

CLAUSE XVI

Continuity of existence, without break or interruption, is the fundamental idea that needs inculcation, not only among children but among ignorant people generally. And the survival, from savage times, of an inclination to associate a full measure of departed personality with the discarded and decomposing bodily remnant,—under the impression that it will awake and live again at some future day,—should be steadily discouraged. The idea of bodily resurrection, in this physical sense, is responsible for much superstition and for some ecclesiastical abuses.

A nearer approach to the truth may be expressed thus :—

Terrestrial existence is dependent for its continuance on a certain arrangement of material particles belonging to the earth, which are gradually collected and built up into the complex and constantly changing structure called a body. The correspondence or connection between matter and spirit, as thus exhibited, is common to every form of life in some degree, and is probably a symbol or sample of something permanently true; so that a double aspect of every fundamental existence is likely always to continue. But identity of person in no way depends upon identity of particles: the particles are frequently changed and the old ones discarded.

The term "body" should be explained and emphasised, as connoting anything which is able to manifest feelings, emotions, and thoughts, and at the same time to operate efficiently on its environment. The temporary character of the present human body should be admitted for purposes of religion; it usefully and truthfully displays the incarnate part of us during the brief episode of terrestrial life, and when it has served its turn it is left behind, its particles being discarded and dispersed. Hereafter —we are taught—an equally efficient vehicle of manifestation, similarly appropriate to our new environment, will not be lacking; this at present unknown and hypothetical entity is spoken of as "a spiritual body," and represents the serious idea underlying crude popular notions about bodily resurrection.

The *ego* has been likened to a ripple raised by wind upon water, displaying in visible form the motion and influence of the operating breath, without being permanently differentiated from the vast whole, of which each ripple is a temporarily individualised portion: individualised, yet not isolated from others, but connected with them by the ocean, of whose immensity it may be supposed for poetic purposes gradually to become aware:—

> "But that one ripple on the boundless deep
> Feels that the deep is boundless, and itself
> For ever changing form, but evermore
> One with the boundless motion of the deep."

There is much to be said for some form of doctrine of a common psychological basis or union of minds—some kind of Anima Mundi, some World-Mind, of which we are all fragments, and to which all knowledge is in a manner accessible; but the analogy of ocean ripples or icebergs need not be pressed to support the idea of a cessation of individual existence, when a given ripple or a given iceberg subsides. All analogies fail at some point. The ocean analogy happens to suggest indistinguishable absorption, or Nirvana, but others do not. The parts of a jelly are linked together and vibrate as a whole, but each little sac of fluid is partitioned off as an individual entity; in touch with all the rest, but with a texture and a colour of its own.

Continued personality, persistent individual existence, cannot be predicated of things which do not possess personality or individuality or character: but, to things which do possess these attributes, continuity and persistence not only may, but must, apply; unless we are to suppose that actual existence suddenly ceases. There must be a conservation of character; notwithstanding the admitted return of the individual to a central store or larger self, from which a portion was differentiated and individualised for the brief period during which the planet performs some seventy of its innumerable journeys round the sun. Absorption in original source may mask, but need not destroy, identity.

Even so a villager, picked out as a recruit and sent to the seat of war, may serve his country, may gain experience, acquire a soul and a width of horizon such as he had not dreamt of; and when he returns, after the war is over, may be merged as before in his native village. But the village is the richer for his presence, and his individuality or personality is not really lost; though to the eye of the world, which has no further need for it, it has practically ceased to be.

The character and experience gained by us during our brief association with the matter of this planet, become our possession henceforth for ever. We cannot shake ourselves free of them, even if we would: the enlargement of ideas, the growth in knowledge, the acquisition of friendships, the skill and power and serviceableness attained by us through this strange experience of incarnation, all persist as part and parcel of our larger self; and so do the memories of failure, of shame, of cruelty, of sin, which we have acquired here. To glory in these last things is damnation: the best that they can bring to us is pain and undying remorse—their worm dieth not and the fire is not quenched. There is no way out, save by the way of mercy and grace; whereby we are assured that at last, in the long last, we may ultimately attain to pardon and peace.

The class of things which is certainly not persistent, but must indubitably be left behind us for ever, is the weird collection of treasures for which most of us work so hard: scorning delights and living laborious days for their acquisition.

In this blind and mistaken struggle—a struggle which in the present condition of society seems so unavoidable, even so meritorious, but which in a reformed society will be looked back upon as at something akin to lunacy—we do not even make to ourselves friends of the mammon of unrighteousness. Its mottoes are "each for himself" and "væ victis." Fortunately very few of the human race wholly succumb to this temptation; nearly all reserve great regions of their lives where kindness and friendliness and affection reign, and try to check the evil results of their worser or self-directed efforts by charitable doles.

In a more ideal state of society there would be no need either of the poison or of its antidote.

To bring about such an ideal state of society is the end and aim of Politics, and of all movements for social reform. Efforts in these directions are the most serious things in life, and may be the most fruitful in vital results: since few individuals are strong enough to withstand the pressure and tendency of their social surroundings. Only a few can rise superior to them, only a few sink far beneath them; the majority drift with the crowd and become—too many at present—irretrievably injured by the base and ugly conditions among which their lives are cast.

At present, for the majority of Englishmen, life is liable to be damaging and deleterious: initial weakness of character, so far from being strengthened and helped by the combined force of society, is hindered and enfeebled thereby,—a disastrous and disquieting condition of things. But when the efforts of self-sacrificing and laborious statesmen, Ministers in the highest sense (Mark x. 43),—when these efforts at cultivation bear fruit,—then, notwithstanding individual lapses here and there, society at large will be indistinguishable from a human branch of the Communion of Saints. Then will feeble impulses towards virtue be fostered and encouraged; the bruised reed will no longer be broken and trampled in the mire.

The Life Eternal in its fullest sense must be entered upon here and now. The emphasis is on the word *Life*, without reference to time. "I am come that ye might have Life." Life of a far higher kind than any we yet know is attainable by the human race on this planet. It rests largely with ourselves. The outlook was never brighter than it is to-day; many workers and thinkers are making ready the way for a Second Advent,—a reincarnation of the Logos in the heart of all men; the heralds are already attuning their songs for a reign of brotherly love; already there are "signs of his coming and sounds of his feet"; and upon our terrestrial activity the date of this Advent depends.

XVII

THE COMMUNION OF SAINTS

Q. 17. *What is the significance of the "Communion of Saints"?*

A. Higher and holier beings must possess, in fuller fruition, those privileges of communion which are already foreshadowed by our own faculties of language, of sympathy, and of mutual aid; and as we find that man's power of friendly help is not confined to his fellows, but extends to other animals, so may we conceive ourselves part of a mighty Fellowship of love and service.

CLAUSE XVII

Here is opened up a great subject on which much remains to be discovered. It is probable that the action of the Deity throughout the Universe is always conducted through intermediaries and agents. In all cases that we can examine, it is so; and this is one of the many meanings of "Immanence."

Humanity is the most prominent, to us, among Divine agencies, and though it is probably only an infinitesimal fraction of the whole, yet it can be studied as a sample. Experience shows us that human beings have feelings of sympathy, pity, and love, and can be moved to act in certain ways by persistent urging and by definite requests. There is no reason to suppose that this faculty of hearing and answering is limited to our own comparatively lowly stage of existence. Man may be regarded as a germ or indication of far more powerful agencies, of which at present we know very little.

The faculty of communion familiarly possessed by man is not likely to be exhaustive of all possible methods of mental and spiritual intercourse; and, in the undeveloped power of telepathy, we have an indication of a mode apparently not dependent on the machinery of physical processes, and not necessarily limited to intelligences inhabiting the surface of a planet. Why associate mind only with the surface of a mass of matter? Enthusiasts hope some day to be able to communicate with people on Mars, but there may be intelligences far more accessible to us than those remote and hypothetical denizens of another world. The immanent Spirit of nature is likely to individualise and personify itself in ways mysterious and unknown: all manner of possibilities lie open to our study and examination; and—until we have scrutinised the evidence, and thought long and deeply on the subject—our negative opinion, based upon long habit and tradition, must not be allowed undue weight. It must be remembered that the above is speculation, not knowledge; yet something like it has received the sanction of great philosophers. Here is an exclamation of Hegel:—

"We do not mean to be behind; our watchword shall be Reason and Freedom, and our rallying ground the Invisible Church."

So far our eyes are open to perceive only the assiduous operations of man; and any supposed influence of other agencies we regard with suspicion and mistrust. Some are inclined to think that man is solitary in the universe, the highest of created things; without equal, without superior, without companionship; alone with his indomitable soul amid scenes of unspeakable grandeur and awe; alone with his brethren in a universe wherein no spark of feeling, no gleam of intelligence, can be aroused by his unuttered longings, no echo of sympathy can respond to his bewildered need.

Yet that is not the feeling which arises during spells of lonely communion with nature, on rock or sea or trackless waste. At these moments comes a sense of Presence, such as Wordsworth felt at Tintern, or Byron when he wrote:

> "Then stirs the feeling infinite, so felt
> In solitude, where we are *least* alone."

Until our senses are opened more widely, scepticism concerning spiritual beings, as intermediate links with absolute Deity, may be our safest attitude, for ignorance is better than superstition; but the seers of the human race have surmised that as denizens of a higher universe we are far from lonely, that it is only our limited perception that is at fault, and that to clearer eyes the whole of nature is transfused with spirit: ἡ ψυχὴ τῷ ὅλῳ μέμικται,

> "Whose dwelling is the light of setting suns,
> And the round ocean and the living air,
> And the blue sky, and in the mind of man."

XVIII

MYSTIC COMMUNION OR PRAYER

Q. 18. *What do you understand by prayer?*

A. I understand that when our spirits are attuned to the Spirit of Righteousness, our hopes and aspirations exert an influence far beyond their conscious range, and in a true sense bring us into communion with our Heavenly Father. This power of filial communion is called prayer; it is an attitude of mingled worship and supplication; we offer petitions in a spirit of trust and submission, and endeavour to realise the Divine attributes, with the help and example of Christ.

CLAUSE XVIII

In prayer we come into close communion with a Higher than we know, and seek to contemplate Divine perfection. Its climax and consummation is attained when we realise the universal Permeance, the entire Goodness, and the Fatherly Love, of the Divine Being. Through prayer we admit our dependence on a Higher Power, for existence and health and everything we possess; we are encouraged to ask for whatever we need, as children ask parents; and we inevitably cry for mercy and comfort in times of tribulation and anguish.

The spirit of simple supplication may desire chiefly—

1. Insight and receptiveness to truth and knowledge.

2. Help and guidance in the practical management of life.

3. Ability and willingness to follow the light whithersoever it leads.

But provided we ask in a right spirit, it is not necessary to be specially careful concerning the kind of things asked for; nor need we in all cases attempt to decide how far their attainment is possible or not. In such matters we may admit our ignorance. What is important is that we should apply our own efforts towards the fulfilment of our petition, and not be satisfied with wishes alone. Everything accomplished has to be done by actual work and activity of some kind, and it is unreasonable to expect the rest of the universe to take trouble on our behalf while we ourselves are supine. Certain material means are within our control: these should be fully employed, in the light of the best knowledge of the time.

The highest type of prayer has for its object not any material benefit, beyond those necessary for our activity and usefulness, but the enlightenment and amendment of our wills, the elevation of all humanity, and the coming of the Kingdom.

XIX

THE LORD'S PRAYER

Q. Rehearse the prayer taught us by Jesus.

A. OUR FATHER WHICH ART IN HEAVEN,

HALLOWED BE THY NAME.

THY KINGDOM COME.

THY WILL BE DONE IN EARTH, AS IT IS IN HEAVEN.

GIVE US THIS DAY OUR DAILY BREAD.

AND FORGIVE US OUR TRESPASSES, AS WE FORGIVE THEM THAT TRESPASS AGAINST US.

AND LEAD US NOT INTO TEMPTATION; BUT DELIVER US FROM EVIL:

FOR THINE IS THE KINGDOM

AND THE POWER,

AND THE GLORY,

FOR EVER.

CLAUSE XIX

Q. 19. *Explain the purport of this prayer.*

A. We first attune our spirit to consciousness of the Divine Fatherhood; trying to realise His infinite holiness as well as His loving-kindness, desiring that everything alien to His will should cease in our hearts and in the world, and longing for the establishment of the Kingdom of Heaven. Then we ask for the supply of the ordinary needs of existence, and for the forgiveness of our sins and shortcomings as we pardon those who have hurt us. We pray to be kept from evil influences, and to be protected when they attack us. Finally, we repose in the might, majesty, and dominion of the Eternal Goodness.

XX

THE KINGDOM OF HEAVEN

Q. 20. *What is meant by the Kingdom of Heaven?*

A. The Kingdom of Heaven is the central feature of practical Christianity. It represents a harmonious condition in which the Divine Will is perfectly obeyed; it signifies the highest state of existence, both individual and social, which we can conceive. Our whole effort should, directly or indirectly, make ready its way,—in our hearts, in our lives, and in the lives of others. It is the ideal state of society towards which Reformers are striving; it is the ideal of conscious existence towards which Saints aim.

CLAUSE XX

This mighty ideal has many aspects. It has been typified as the pearl of great price, for which all other possessions may well be sacrificed: in germ it is as leaven, or as growing seed. It will come sooner than is expected, though for a time longer there must be tares among the wheat: for a time longer there shall be last and first, and a striving to be greatest, and a laying up of earthly treasure, and wars and divisions; but only for a time,—the spirit of service is growing, and the childlike spirit will overcome:

"Fear not, little flock; for it is your Father's good pleasure to give you the Kingdom."

When realised, it will conduce to universal love and brotherhood; it is the reign of Christ's spirit in the hearts of all men; it is accordingly spoken of as the second Advent, and its herald song is still, Peace on earth, goodwill among men. Wherever perfect love and willing service exist, there already is the Kingdom.

We have to realise that the Will of God is to be done on earth, that the Kingdom of Heaven is to be a present Kingdom, here and now, not relegated indefinitely to the future. Our life is not in the future, but in the present, and it will always be in the present: it is in our life that we have to apply our beliefs, utilise our talents, and bring forth fruit. The Kingdom of Heaven is not only at hand, it is potentially in our midst, and may be actually within us. These are its two chief aspects, the social, and the individual. The ideal is to be made real, in each and in all: nothing is too good to be true: each soul is to attain its highest aim: the world is to be transfigured and transformed.

The above formula must not be supposed to exhaust the meaning of the great Phrase, which many parables have still only partially explained, but it is a part of its meaning. And the strange thing is that the world, with all its competition, wrestling and contending amid unheeded calls to order, is really working towards that goal. No other ending is possible in the long run, though it has been long delayed. It is the condition towards which the whole of humanity, each individual man, as well as the race, is blindly and unconsciously struggling;

> "Their prejudice and fears and cares and doubts
> All with a touch of nobleness; despite
> Their error, upward tending all, though weak,
> Like plants in mines which never saw the sun,
> But dream of him and guess where he may be,
> And do their best to climb and get to him."

The daily toil, in city office, in factory, in ship, in mine, in home, is really a struggle for Life, for freedom, for joy, for something wider and better than we at present know, for pleasures that satisfy and do not pall. We needs must love the highest when we see it, but as yet we do not see it: so we are working in the dark, and the best of us try hard to do our duty. The end is unrecognised, the means may be mistaken, but the energy is there; and the race as well as the individual is instinctively working out its destiny;—thwarting itself constantly by misdirected endeavour, yet constantly striving for self-development and enlargement, for progress and happiness. And this is true even when the main idea of enlargement is the amassing of money in unwieldy heaps, when happiness is sought in an exaltation of imagination by deleterious drugs, or when progress is thought to consist in the slaughter and impoverishment of opponents who might be our auxiliaries and allies.

If our vision could be cleared, and the aim of human effort could be changed, the earth would put on a new complexion; we should no longer be tempted to think of humanity as of an ancient and effete and played-out product of evolution,—we the latest-born and most youthful of all the creatures on the planet,—but should regard everything with the eye of hope, as of one new born, with senses quickened to perceive joys and beauties hitherto undreamt of.

That is the meaning of Regeneration or new birth: it must be like an awakening out of trance. At present we are as if subject to a dream illusion, in a slumber which we are unable to throw off. Revelation after revelation has come to us, but our senses are deadened and we will not hear, our hands are full of clay, we have no grasp for ideals, we are mistaking appearance for reality. But the time for awakening must be drawing nigh—the time when again it may be said: "The people that walked in darkness have seen a great light: they that dwell in the land of the shadow of death, upon them hath the light shined."

Meanwhile our seers depict man's half-hoping half-despairing attitude, not so much as a striving, as a waiting:—the striving is obvious, but the unconscious waiting is what they detect—waiting as it were for the arrival of a new sense, a new perception of the value of life:—

> "And we, the poor earth's dying race, and yet
> No phantoms, watching from a phantom shore
> Await the last and largest sense to make
> The phantom walls of this illusion fade,
> And show us that the world is wholly fair."

THE CLAUSES OF THE CATECHISM REPEATED

THE CATECHISM

Q. 1. *What are you?*

A. I am a being alive and conscious upon this earth, a descendant of ancestors who rose by gradual processes from lower forms of animal life, and with struggle and suffering became man.

Q. 2. *What, then, may be meant by the Fall of man?*

A. At a certain stage of development man became conscious of a difference between right and wrong, so that thereafter, when his actions fell below a normal standard of conduct, he felt ashamed and sinful. He thus lost his animal innocency, and entered on a long period of human effort and failure; nevertheless, the consciousness of degradation marked a rise in the scale of existence.

Q. 3. *What is the distinctive character of manhood?*

A. The distinctive character of man is that he has a sense of responsibility for his acts, having acquired the power of choosing between good and evil, with freedom to obey one motive rather than another. Creatures far below the human level are irresponsible; they feel no shame and suffer no remorse; they are said to have no conscience.

Q. 4. *What is the duty of man?*

A. To assist his fellows, to develop his own higher self, to strive towards good in every way open to his powers, and generally to seek to know the laws of Nature and to obey the will of God; in whose service alone can be found that harmonious exercise of the faculties which is identical with perfect freedom.

Q. 5. *What is meant by good and evil?*

A. Good is that which promotes development, and is in harmony with the will of God. It is akin to health and beauty and happiness.

Evil is that which retards or frustrates development, and injures some part of the universe. It is akin to disease and ugliness and misery.

Q. 6. *How does man know good from evil?*

A. His own nature, when uncorrupted by greed, is sufficiently in harmony with the rest of the universe to enable him to be well aware in general of what is a help or a hindrance to the guiding Spirit, of which he himself is a real and effective portion.

Q. 7. *How comes it that evil exists?*

A. Evil is not an absolute thing, but has reference to a standard of attainment. The possibility of evil is the necessary consequence of a rise in the scale of moral existence; just as an organism whose normal temperature is far above "absolute zero" is necessarily liable to damaging and deadly cold. But cold is not in itself a positive or created thing.

Q. 8. *What is sin?*

A. Sin is the deliberate and wilful act of a free agent who sees the better and chooses the worse, and thereby acts injuriously to himself and others. The root sin is selfishness, whereby needless trouble and pain are inflicted on others; when fully developed it involves moral suicide.

Q. 9. *Are there beings lower in the scale of existence than man?*

A. Yes, multitudes. In every part of the earth where life is possible, there we find it developed. Life exists in every variety of animal, in earth and air and sea, and in every species of plant.

Q. 10. *Are there any beings higher in the scale of existence than man?*

A. Man is the highest of the dwellers on the planet earth, but the earth is only one of many planets warmed by the sun, and the sun is only one of a myriad of similar suns, which are so far off that we barely see them and group them indiscriminately as "stars." We may reasonably conjecture that in some of the innumerable worlds circling round those distant suns there must be beings far higher in the scale of existence than ourselves; indeed, we have no knowledge which enables us to assert the absence of intelligence anywhere.

Q. 11. *What caused and what maintains existence?*

A. Of our own knowledge we are unable to realise the meaning of origination or of maintenance; all that we ourselves can accomplish in the physical world is to move things into desired positions, and leave them to act on each other. Nevertheless our effective movements are inspired by thought, and so we conceive that Intelligence is immanent in all the processes of nature; for they are not random and purposeless, but organised and beautiful.

Q. 12. *What is to be said of man's higher faculties?*

A. The faculties and achievements of the highest among mankind—in Art, in Science, in Philosophy, and in Religion—are not explicable as an outcome of a struggle for existence. Something more than mere life is possessed by us—something represented by the words "mind" and "soul" and "spirit." On one side we are members of the animal kingdom; on another we are associates in a loftier type of existence, and are linked with the Divine

Q. 13. *Is man helped in his struggle upward?*

A. There is a Power in the Universe vastly beyond our comprehension; and we trust and believe that it is a Good and Loving Power, able and willing to help us and all creatures, and to guide us wisely, without detriment to our incipient freedom. This Loving-kindness continually surrounds us; in it we live and have our real being; it is the mainspring of joy and love and beauty, and we call it the Grace of God. It sustains and enriches all worlds, and may take a multiplicity of forms, but it was specially manifested to dwellers on this planet in the Life of Jesus Christ, through whose spirit and living influence the race of man may hope to rise to heights at present inaccessible.

Q. 14. *How may we become informed concerning things too high for our own knowledge?*

A. We should strive to learn from the great teachers, the prophets and poets and saints of the human race, and should seek to know and to interpret their inspired writings.

Q. 15. *What, then, do you reverently believe can be deduced from a study of the records and traditions of the past in the light of the present?*

A. I believe in one Infinite and Eternal Being a guiding and loving Father, in whom all things consist.

I believe that the Divine Nature is specially revealed to man through Jesus Christ our Lord, who lived and taught and suffered in Palestine 1900 years ago, and has since been worshipped by the Christian

Church as the immortal Son of God, the Saviour of the world.

I believe that the Holy Spirit is ever ready to help us along the Way towards Goodness and Truth; that prayer is a means of communion between man and God; and that it is our privilege through faithful service to enter into the Life Eternal, the Communion of Saints, and the Peace of God.

Q. 16. *What do you mean by the Life Eternal?*

A. I mean that whereas our terrestrial existence is temporary, our real existence continues without ceasing, in either a higher or a lower form, according to our use of opportunities and means of grace; and that the fulness of Life ultimately attainable represents a growing perfection at present inconceivable by us.

Q. 17. *What is the significance of "the Communion of Saints"?*

A. Higher and holier beings must possess, in fuller fruition, those privileges of communion which are already foreshadowed by our own faculties of language, of sympathy, and of mutual aid; and as we know that man's power of friendly help is not confined to his fellows, but extends to other animals, so may we conceive ourselves part of a mighty Fellowship of love and service.

Q. 18. *What do you understand by prayer?*

A. I understand that when our spirits are attuned to the Spirit of Righteousness, our hopes and aspirations exert an influence far beyond their conscious range, and in a true sense bring us into communion with our Heavenly Father. This power of filial communion is called prayer; it is an attitude of mingled worship and supplication; we offer petitions in a spirit of trust and submission, and endeavour to realise the Divine attributes, with the help and example of Christ.

Q. Rehearse the prayer taught us by Jesus.

A. Our Father, etc.

Q. 19. *Explain the clauses of this prayer.*

A. We first attune our spirit to consciousness of the Divine Fatherhood; trying to realise His infinite holiness as well as His loving-kindness, desiring that everything alien to His will should cease in our hearts and in the world, and longing for the establishment of the Kingdom of Heaven. Then we ask for the supply of the ordinary needs of existence, and for the forgiveness of our sins and shortcomings as we pardon those who have hurt us. We pray to be kept from evil influences, and to be protected when they attack us. Finally, we repose in the might, majesty, and dominion of the Eternal Goodness.

Q. 20. *What is meant by the Kingdom of Heaven?*

A. The Kingdom of Heaven is the central feature of practical Christianity. It represents a harmonious condition in which the Divine Will is perfectly obeyed; it signifies the highest state of existence, both individual and social, which we can conceive. Our whole effort should, directly or indirectly, make ready its way,—in our hearts, in our lives, and in the lives of others. It is the ideal state of society towards which Reformers are striving; it is the ideal of conscious existence towards which Saints aim.